For the Love
of Therapy

FOR THE LOVE OF THERAPY

CULTIVATING DEEPER JOY, PASSION, AND
AUTHENTICITY IN YOUR PRACTICE

NICOLE ARZT AND JEREMY ARZT

For the Love of Therapy

To Bryson and Logan
We love you more than the whole sky and all the stars.

CONTENTS

INTRODUCTION

We began writing this book in 2022, and it took many different shapes over the past two years. Throughout the process, we talked to hundreds of therapists and clients of therapy, combed through countless statistics, and spent hours musing to each other about what it means to be a therapist.

We intended to write a book for therapists who want to enjoy their work but feel weighed down by disillusionment, discouragement, incompetence, or burnout. Maybe, like many mental health professionals, you feel like you move through your days carrying a burden of fatigue or cynicism. Perhaps you struggle with feeling like you either care too much or not enough about your work. The toughest parts of the job may evoke immense angst, leading you to ask yourself those tough existential questions like *Am I helping my clients? Is any of this making a difference? What do those other professional, put-together therapists seem to have that I don't? Is being a therapist really for me?*

We set out to answer some of these questions by diving

into research. We sifted through many studies about psychotherapy, poring through articles on self-disclosure, therapeutic alliances, and compassion fatigue. We value the data and share many of our findings throughout the book. Our original intention was to create a manual presenting the most accurate, updated research about how to enjoy being an effective modern-day therapist.

However, the more we gathered information and summarized data, the more questions arose that led us to believe that some therapists' experiences were underrepresented or missing altogether. We kept asking ourselves, *Okay, but . . .* Okay, those results are interesting, but who were those therapists in that sample size? Okay, that therapy protocol worked, but who exactly were those clients? Okay, but what confounding variables affected these results? Okay, those findings seem promising, but they don't necessarily match how our colleagues or clients feel about this issue.

Let us ask: Do you feel represented in modern research about the psychotherapy career? Have you ever participated in a study about your professional work? Do you believe that the current research encapsulates the nuances of the therapy you provide your clients?

Maybe. Maybe not.

A discrepancy between hard research and clinical application exists. Real-life therapy will always feel different from how textbooks or research articles describe treatment. Real-life therapy can be spontaneous and fluid and jagged. Real-life clients are more robust and complex than the one-dimensional clients usually featured in vignettes. Therapy happens in offices and on computer screens, in playgrounds and homes, in classrooms, and on nature walks. Treatment can last one session or three hundred sessions, and that session can be free or may cost hundreds of dollars. It can be manualized, eclectic, somatic, or experiential. Clients can struggle with anxiety, distractibility, childhood trauma, underemployment, psychosis, gambling, or a neighbor's aggression. They are three years old and they are eighty-three years old. Even with their treatment goals in place, clients are always whole people with elaborate personalities that are far too complex to ever capture in a research study.

Of course, research matters. Good data shapes efficacy, and it legitimizes the much-needed science part of therapy. But all studies have their limits. Our book blends statistics with storytelling. Our particular type of storytelling entailed holding real conversations with real therapists in the real world.

We spoke to anyone who wanted to talk, including colleagues, mentors, and professors. We turned to social media, where, at the time of this writing, Nicole's @psychotherapymemes page on Instagram has amassed an audience of more than 160,000 mental health professionals. This diverse community of new and seasoned clinicians eagerly shared their candid experiences. We found that many people wanted to talk—and we hope we spoke to people like you.

We were not surprised to find that intense dismay pervades our profession. Many providers feel tired, burnt out, disrespected, unappreciated, apathetic, anxious, and unsure whether they are suited for the career. They often care deeply about their clients, but the constraints of feeling overworked and unsupported impact their capacity for care. And if you've ever had an agonizing day at work, you know firsthand how a challenging client dynamic can call your entire identity into question.

Many books are devoted to the nuts and bolts of

conducting therapy. It often seems as if the authors of these books adhere to a similar outline: they present their theory and then share a brilliant transcript showcasing masterful intervention with impressive client receptiveness. We have read so many of these books throughout our careers. They ooze with impact, encouraging us to think differently and try to apply that same expertise to our own clinical practices.

Okay, but.

Do those vignettes apply to you and your work? Does it feel as if those authors are writing to *you*?

What if you're a tired associate who sees a hundred-plus clients a month? What if you're a school therapist facilitating sessions in an empty classroom or on the playground? What if you haven't had much training but still must meet with your clients despite feeling woefully incompetent? What if your supervisor doesn't care what you're doing with clients, but your job is on the line because you haven't met unrealistic productivity standards?

Are those books duping us all? Or is this just one gripe associated with most literature aimed at therapists? The truth is that most graduate schools, training programs, and books are conducted with a significant slant toward *one kind of therapist*. This therapist is generally a cash-pay private practice provider with complete control over their clientele. When these therapists write books, they typically highlight two types of clients: insightful clients who are fully invested in their therapy process, or apprehensive clients who become invested after one or two masterfully executed interventions.

Of course, these therapist-authors have much knowledge to offer. Many of them trained under renowned researchers and clinicians. Some are tenured professors who have founded institutes. They have created evidence-based theories and have published hundreds of articles. They are unquestionably skilled and sought after. They are impressive and moving and are pioneering important work in this field.

Okay, but.

Something is missing in all of this, isn't it? Maybe you resonate with that feeling of disconnect. Maybe you feel like there's this unspoken chasm between all that's been written about therapy versus who you actually are as a therapist. That's why we need more conversations that speak to the many therapists who feel underrepresented or downright invisible in our field.

If this speaks to you, we believe you're part of this profession's collective majority. You may not have it all figured out, but you're trying your best. These are the therapists we talk to every day. We have supervised and taught these therapists. We see them as clients in our own practices. They have attended our workshops and clinical trainings. They are our colleagues and dear friends, and they are devoted to providing impactful work.

Okay, but who are we?

Our first role in writing this book is our role as therapists. Between us, we've held positions in hospitals, nonprofit organizations, school settings, community mental health, inpatient treatment, and now private practice. At different points, we've managed high caseloads and earned dismal salaries. We know the grinding pressure of meeting productivity goals and accruing hours toward licensure. We've both experienced the drudgery of burnout, and many of our colleagues struggle with it too. The heartache among therapists is real. We have felt it. We observe it everywhere. We write all about it in these pages.

We also wear a few other professional hats. Jeremy has worked as an adjunct faculty member, clinical director, and supervisor for training therapists for several years. Nicole authored *Sometimes Therapy Is Awkward* in 2020 and continues to write for many large publications. She is also known for her humorous and relatable @psychotherapymemes page, which has become a community for therapists around the world. We both have conducted many trainings and workshops on themes of imposter syndrome, burnout, and the realities of working as modern-day therapists.

Despite wearing all the other hats, our hearts always gravitate most toward the relational work of therapy. The richness of this experience is unparalleled. It is an honor to hold space for clients. If you are a past or current client reading this, please know how much we sincerely care for you—then, now, and for the rest of our lives. Thank you for letting us walk with you on your journeys.

While we hope the ideas here transcend a specific theory, it feels important to mention that our therapeutic work is largely person-centered, attachment-based, and psychodynamic. These themes also heavily influence our writing, and you will note them throughout. Building authentic and deeply connected relationships with our clients is the core of what makes this work so meaningful to us.

We are a married couple. We have two children. We have been and are clients of therapy ourselves. Like most therapists, we are complex individuals with unique mental health histories. In our bones, we believe good therapy is transformational, which is why we care so passionately about the profession.

We do not assume an expert stance because we are not experts. Instead, we pose challenging questions, share insights, offer validation, and encourage deeper introspection. However, our goal, as therapists and as writers, is *not* to tell people what to do. Instead, we offer various takeaways that might provide a road map to help you build more confidence and competence in your career.

RISKS AND BENEFITS OF READING THIS BOOK

We first hope that you feel supported and seen. As therapists, we know the mere act of being seen can be one of the most pivotal parts of treatment. Many people move through life feeling misunderstood, and it is powerful to feel witnessed. You are not alone in your struggles. This profession is riddled with many structural problems, which we discuss in detail. We also hope that, regardless of your circumstances, our book offers some strategies for reigniting or cultivating more passion for your work.

The risks mirror the main risks of therapy. Cultivating insight can feel unnerving, causing you to initially feel overwhelmed or angry. You may confront some difficult realities about yourself or your work as you read. Reconciling such awareness can be difficult, but denial also comes with its own steep costs. Change is hard, and not changing is also hard. We deeply validate the convoluted emotions associated with both experiences.

HOW THIS BOOK IS ORGANIZED

For the Love of Therapy is divided into three parts: Part I dives into the reasons many therapists feel insecure or incompetent in their work. Part II moves into specific client concerns and introduces our CHAIR model, which highlights the merits of consistency, hope, attunement, impact, and repair. Part III addresses burnout, compensation concerns, and the existential realities of being a therapist.

All three parts connect, but not every suggestion or

difficulty will apply to you. We trust you will take the insights you need and gently leave the rest. Although we feel dedicated to preserving the integrity of therapy, we sometimes miss the mark. If any of our writing comes across as insensitive or ignorant, we welcome that feedback and will do our best to integrate it into our work moving forward.

Therapy, theories, and interventions evolve, and we recognize that certain ways of thinking become outdated. This book should not be used as a substitute for your own learning, supervision, or personal therapy. Instead, it is a presentation of data coupled with actionable strategies for strengthening your joy and competence in your work.

We see therapists who feel lost and stuck and unsure about how to help their clients. We hear the frustration and confusion that come with doubting this career path. We feel the collective experience of imposter syndrome that affects people in our profession.

There is a heaviness. There is fear and doubt and anger. And many books just don't address these emotions.

You matter. Your work matters.

Regardless of where you are, whether you're questioning your career choice, whether your insecurities have you doubting your competence entirely, or whether you're in the thick of burnout, we wrote our book for *you*.

Finally, although we debated various options, we named this book *For the Love of Therapy* because, ultimately, the word *love* felt most congruent to our philosophy and our mission. Our deepest hope is that our writing helps you cultivate more love in your work as a therapist.

PART I

UNPACKING YOUR INSECURITY AND UNEASE

CHAPTER 1

HAS THE THERAPY PROFESSION FAILED YOU?

Are you happy in this profession? Do you enjoy going to work, meeting with your clients, and embodying the role of a therapist?

If not, why not? Here is a checklist of statements that may apply to your current circumstances. Which ones sound familiar to you?

- You don't feel confident in your therapeutic skills.
- You don't feel adequately supported by your supervisor or colleagues.
- You have too many clients on your caseload.
- You aren't being compensated adequately for your work.
- You feel burnt out.
- You're being asked to perform tasks beyond your scope of competence.
- You're overwhelmed with issues happening in your personal life.

- You don't like some or many of your clients.
- You feel overwhelmed by all the certifications and trainings available to you.
- You're constantly worried about making a mistake that could affect your entire career.
- You're feeling hopeless about your clients or humanity in general.

If any of these concerns resonate with you, you're not alone. In fact, if you have never identified with any of these issues, we'd consider you an anomaly in this profession. Throughout this book, we unpack how these barriers affect therapists. We also offer applicable strategies for managing those barriers as they apply to your *current* life and career circumstances.

The title of this chapter is "Has the Therapy Profession Failed You?" Like the word *love, failure* is also a strong word. But the question is worth asking, isn't it? As noted earlier, many providers are unhappy in their careers. Many also feel insecure about their competence and ability to support their clients. Professional burnout also represents a serious and common problem among therapists.

It's too simplistic to suggest that this is a *you* problem. It's not necessarily about *you* not being smart or experienced enough to do this work. It's also not just about *you* not doing enough self-care. In reality, numerous structural issues impede competence. Subsequently, the actual role of being a therapist is complex and subjective. At times, it's just downright confusing to know what to do with clients. Let's address some of the main problems.

PROBLEM: THERAPISTS ARE SIMULTANEOUSLY "IN DEMAND" AND UNDERVALUED

The topic of mental health is often at the forefront of our modern sociopolitical conversation; the trope is that therapists are *in demand*, and with good reason. Here are some startling statistics we gathered in 2023: The World Health Organization reported a 13% rise in mental health disorders and substance use disorders in the last decade.[1] It's estimated that the impact of depression and anxiety costs the global economy US $1 trillion per year.[2] In addition, approximately 132 Americans die by suicide each day.[3] And 1 in 6 US children between ages two and eight have a diagnosed developmental or mental health condition.[4] Statistics show that 7 out of 10 adults have experienced at least some kind of traumatic event, and an American is sexually assaulted every 68 seconds.[5] Approximately 1 in 5 people currently take a prescribed psychiatric medication, at least 1 out of every 10 people will meet the criteria for an alcohol use disorder, and more than 10,000 people die each year from symptoms related to eating disorders.[6]

Amid these overwhelming statistics, people are advised to *go to therapy*, as if we therapists hold some elusive, surefire remedy for solving all that plagues humanity. Therapists, especially new therapists, are at risk of absorbing a colossal sense of responsibility for "fixing" this crisis.

We're often reminded that there is a shortage of mental health providers. At the time of this writing, many agencies carry long wait lists, and the community mental health system struggles to fill open positions. Back in 2004, 13% of adults reported visiting a mental health professional in the previous year. That number nearly doubled to 23% in 2022.[7] With younger generations exhibiting more receptiveness to mental health treatment, it's likely this figure will continue to rise.

But if we're all in demand, why do so many of us feel undervalued or replaceable? Why are so many beloved colleagues questioning the field altogether? In 2022, Nicole posted a tweet that read, *Shoutout to all the therapists doing sessions in garages, supply closets, playgrounds, pantries, and other unfortunately-we-don't-have-an-office-space-for-you   locations. Your work fucking matters.* That tweet generated more than 25,000 likes on Instagram and continues to be reposted, commented on, and shared worldwide.

This shoutout spoke to the perils of our modern healthcare industry. It's no secret that our profession is fraught with exploitative practices that often demand excessive productivity. We talk about this problem extensively in the third part of this book. Exploitation often feels like a standard rite of passage in clinical work. But many therapists feel like new swimmers tossed into a rip current with a distant lifeguard screaming, "Just trust the water!"

The script often resembles this: You care deeply about providing clients with competent and compassionate care. But you may lack the resources, emotional support, and adequate compensation to focus on providing that care. You may be reminded that you don't become a therapist for the money, but do you earn enough to cover your basic needs, student loan repayments, licensing fees, and continuing education to stay relevant in the field?

Do you feel valued for the hard work you provide? Maybe. Maybe not.

This book certainly can't fix the feeling of being undervalued. However, we attempt to validate this frustrating experience and offer insights about how to feel empowered despite this phenomenon.

PROBLEM: IT'S HARD TO DEFINE HOW THERAPY "SHOULD" LOOK

What are therapists supposed to do with their clients? It depends on whom you ask. Your supervisor or mentor may say one thing. The insurance company authorizing treatment will say something else. And, of course, your actual client may have a different take on what they need and what you offer them. The profession has become as varied and flexible as the clients it treats. While this sounds freeing, it poses significant challenges.

It wasn't always this way. For many years, therapy was almost exclusively practiced by white men with other white, wealthy folk. Offering therapy to the mainstream masses is still in its infancy stage. And today's therapists come from all different backgrounds and life experiences.

With dozens of treatment modalities to choose from, how do we choose what's best? Do we ask clients about their relationship with their mother? Encourage them to identify what they feel in their body? Offer a worksheet to help them understand their automatic thoughts? Help them practice asserting boundaries with their overbearing colleague? Request that they draw a picture representing their fear? You get the idea.

And how do we know the "correct" diagnosis? The DSM dates back to 1952, when only 106 options were available. The latest edition, the DSM-5-TR, published in 2022, contains nearly three hundred diagnoses. While some clients need treatment to manage a specific diagnosis, many also want support for a myriad of other presenting concerns, ranging from low self-esteem to childhood cyberbullying to career ambivalence to acute grief.

As a society, we've unquestionably raised awareness about

the importance of mental health treatment. Therapy has evolved into a popular, frontline option, and this is a good thing. But has the definition become so broad as to be meaningless? Therapy is often recommended to *anyone* with seemingly *any* presenting issue.

Within this matrix, again, how are we supposed to know what to do when we're sitting with a client?

Let's say you graduated with a good working knowledge of theories, practice strategies, laws, and ethics. You read many case vignettes and treatment transcripts; you spent time in class exploring why people do what they do and how they can change. You discussed which methods can best support clients given their presenting concerns.

Then you were thrust into real-life therapy with real-life people with a wide assortment of problems. And your clients, who are three-dimensional humans instead of characters in a vignette, feel so much different than the transcripts. Maybe you sometimes feel anchored by vague affirmations, such as *It's an art, and you don't have to do it perfectly. Just be yourself! Just be a human. Trust the process!* You have likely been told you will learn by practicing, by spending hours and hours sitting with different clients. You have also been told you'll eventually get a feel for the work, and to follow your intuition.

But should you really trust those affirmations without having an accurate baseline for what therapy should look like? The stakes are high. Clients are trusting you with their secrets, fears, and emotional wellness. What if you get it wrong? What if you cause harm?

It might seem like you're on your own to figure it out. And you might feel totally lost.

In this way, the therapy profession differs greatly from many other industries in which apprenticeship represents a core feature of training. Consider this: Would you want to receive a haircut from a barber who learned to cut hair only by watching a few tutorials and reading a book? Would you hire a brand-new roofer to replace your home's roof without any on-site supervision? Would you choose a surgeon to perform a procedure if they had never observed that particular procedure before?

No, you wouldn't. We certainly wouldn't either. These specific scenarios sound inconceivable. In other fields, novices perform work with direct supervision *on the scene*. Their training is explicit and concrete. Within these sectors, both professionals and consumers recognize that on-the-job training is part of building mastery. It's assumed the trainee will extensively shadow and be shadowed by the professional.

But how many times have you watched other therapists conduct therapy? And how many times have other therapists watched you work?

Probably not many. If you're like most therapists, you've spent infinitely more time doing therapy than observing therapy. You've also probably spent many, many hours sitting alone with clients without receiving any specific feedback or direction to help refine your craft.

This leads us to our next problem.

PROBLEM: WE HAVEN'T CONCRETELY DEFINED COMPETENCE

Clinical licensing boards require that therapists adhere to their scope of competence. According to their standards, you shouldn't treat clients whose issues exceed your area of expertise. In theory, this concept sounds appropriate. But what does it definitively mean?

First, how is competence attained? And when can you confidently state that you are fit to provide treatment for a certain client? If you aren't sure, you're in good company. There isn't a great working definition of therapeutic competence.

For example, is it ethical to treat a client if you've never worked with their presenting diagnosis? Maybe not. But what if you're seeking active consultation around the case? Or what if you meet with a supervisor who has extensive experience treating that kind of issue? What about if you're currently in a training program to become certified to treat clients with that diagnosis? Do any of these actions make you competent? And what if you have worked with your client on an unrelated issue, only to discover this other diagnosis seven months in?

We ask these challenging questions because they speak to the uncertainty so many therapists feel. In many ways, our field lacks tangible parameters for defining competence and skill. If you're like most therapists, you have been assigned a variety of clients without necessarily trusting that you have the proficiency to treat them.

Let's pause here. Take a moment and think about the best therapist you know. Now, spend another moment and answer this question: What exactly makes them the best? Who came to mind? Was it you? Probably not. Was it your favorite theorist? Your supervisor? Your own therapist? An inspirational therapist you follow on social media?

Which metrics did you use to evaluate their excellence? Maybe you considered their personality—perhaps they are warm or intelligent or thoughtful in how they conceptualize therapy. Maybe they are a skillful instructor or gifted author. Perhaps it's more intuitive—you might have an implicit sense that they engage in effective work with their clients. Is excellence measured by their retention rates? Direct client feedback?

Again, we ask, *What makes someone a competent therapist?*

It's hard to answer and even harder for a group of people to answer. To magnify this unique dilemma, let's compare therapists with athletes. Millions of people play basketball, but only the top players ever compete in the NBA. There is no randomness or guessing. Every player's skill is observable and quantifiable. Nobody accidentally makes it to the NBA, regardless of how dedicated or knowledgeable about basketball they are. The best athletes in any sport rise to the top, and they must maintain their level of excellence to remain on the top.

When it comes to discerning your therapeutic skills, how do you know where you land in a lineup? Are you in the NBA? Are you just an amateur playing pickup ball? Somewhere in between? And where does your favorite teacher or colleague rank? When you reflect on the best therapist you know, would you place them in the therapist equivalent of the NBA? Should our field even have its own NBA?

At this point, you might say, *But therapy is subjective! It is not anything like basketball.*

And you would be correct. Of course, therapy isn't basketball. The objectives of any team sport are consistently the same: score more points than the other team. Therapy objectives are far more complex and varied. Compared with an athlete, who has a specific set of goals in mind, a therapist's style is infinitely more fluid.

But, as we will discuss in the next chapter, if you don't have clear objectives for building competence, how can you tell if you're improving in your craft? And how can you even assess whether you're actually helping your clients? Without established protocols in place, is it any wonder so many therapists feel insecure and unequipped?

Many people in this profession relate to feeling insecure or incompetent. In 2023, in an Instagram poll, Nicole asked, "Therapists, how often do you feel incompetent in your work?" Out of the 18,700 respondents, 30% said "always or almost always"; 55% said "sometimes"; 12% said "occasionally"; and just 3% said "almost never or never."

So, in this poll, 97% of therapists related to feeling incompetent. Although we're aware that insecure therapists may have been more apt to respond than those who are secure, it's still a sobering number. With so many therapists experiencing incompetence, we can't ignore or downplay this macro-level phenomenon.

Perhaps this is the real undercurrent often confused with imposter syndrome. When therapists acknowledge feeling incompetent, they tend to receive one-dimensional advice about how to fix *themselves*. This advice sounds like *You need to go to supervision and talk about your incompetence. You also need to go to therapy to work on your low self-esteem. And you should practice better self-talk when that inner critic speaks. Don't forget that good listening and having a warm presence is more than enough—who cares if you don't know what you're doing beyond that?!*

Although those suggestions are helpful, they are also shortsighted. More than that, they disregard the reality that most therapists are already working on themselves. You don't just need to cultivate your individual wellness and naively trust that it's an art. You also need established protocols to help you build actual competence. You need ways to measure your work and overall efficacy.

We don't know any therapists who don't care about the

well-being of their clients. But we do know many, many therapists who care and don't exactly know how to help.

Throughout this book, we provide various strategies for strengthening your skill set. In chapter 4, we will also identify what you can specifically do to increase your therapeutic competence.

CHAPTER 2

WHY DO YOU FEEL SO LOST IN YOUR CAREER?

W e've talked about how so many therapists feel confused or scattered about what treatment looks like and how to build competence in this profession.

You may experience feeling scattered internally because you want to help your client as much as you can. You also may be straddling various pressures in other, more external ways. For example, clients desire fast relief, agencies require high productivity, insurance companies demand concrete interventions and results, and the client's family may expect unrealistic miracles to occur.

Where do we focus? How do we decide where to start and what roads to follow?

It's been suggested that the average person makes 35,000 decisions each day. Realistically, though, this number seems impossible to quantify. In 2018, the fast-food franchise Subway advertised that its restaurant menu alone yielded 4.9 billion possible combinations;[1] 4.9 billion is much greater than 35,000, particularly when you factor in that this accounts for only one meal at one restaurant. The point is, whether it's choosing a sandwich bread or a life partner, every moment in time presents an opportunity to accept one option and simultaneously turn down an infinite number of alternatives.

The abundance of choice can lead to *decision fatigue*, which refers to the emotional exhaustion associated with the sheer volume of decisions you make each day. Therapists experiencing decision fatigue struggle to make sound choices and may be prone to impulsivity and feeling perpetually overwhelmed. Decision paralysis, which happens when you feel unable to make a choice altogether, can also occur. This can look like a mental shutdown, and it can take the form of perpetual procrastination or feelings of stuckness. We created the following graphic to demonstrate the interplay of choices therapists weigh each day. Each layer impacts other layers. Decision fatigue or paralysis in one layer can also affect your capacity for making good choices elsewhere.

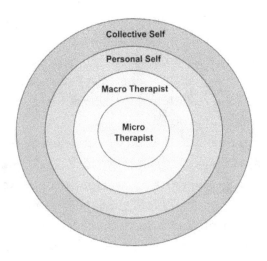

COLLECTIVE SELF

The collective self is the broadest layer and is influenced by culture and society at large. The choices made in this layer are largely automatic and unconscious. For example, American society collectively agrees with the law that drivers must stop at red lights. When you drive, you don't consciously think, *Should I stop at this light?* The requirement to stop has already been stored in your procedural memory, which means you unconsciously remember to stop.

Procedural memory is what allows you to type, ride a bike, or swim without thinking about it. You don't have to consciously decide which action to take. Your body has memorized the motion and rhythm.

Most people automatically adhere to the rules within the collective self. In the case of the traffic light, if you can't or don't comply, you may face steep consequences, including social alienation, financial devastation, legal problems, and even death. We all know the perils associated with running red lights.

Of course, it's worth acknowledging that just because a rule feels implicit doesn't mean it's morally sound. Progressive societal change hinges on people recognizing that automatic choices can be challenged. When enough people question a status quo, significant shifts may occur. For example, if even 10% of drivers chose to disregard red lights, this effect would rapidly change how everyone drove.

PERSONAL SELF

The next layer, the personal self, is also influenced by culture and society. Your individual beliefs, family dynamics, and peer relationships shape the decisions here.

The personal self is where the dilemma of 4.9 billion potential combinations available at Subway lives. Every day, you must make so many choices, such as where you buy gas, when you should make brunch reservations, how much to spend on your kids' teachers' holiday gifts, and whether you want to buy that deodorant or one of the seven thousand other options available to you.

This category is truly limitless, and this is the space where many people experience the fear of missing out (FOMO). How do you settle on one choice when so many options exist? It's also in this space where you can spend years agonizing over gigantic life decisions. Even when you align well with one value, it's incredibly easy to find an argument demonstrating why considering another value may be better. All decisions have consequences, and the weight of those potential consequences can feel overwhelming.

Modern technology has augmented the possibility of choice within the personal self. For instance, before the internet, you might have known only what your immediate community was doing. Now, we can see how everyone in the world lives. We have "expert" advice available to us everywhere. And while having that information can be helpful, the endless volume may feel suffocating.

MACRO THERAPIST SELF

The remaining two layers focus directly on all the choices therapists must make within their profession. In the macro layer are all the decisions associated with structuring your role as a therapist. At every point in this career, you need to consider many options, including:

- Which type of degree should you pursue?

- What kind of company do you want to work for?
- Should you go into private practice?
- How much should you negotiate for your salary?
- What's the optimal way to arrange the furniture in your office?
- Do you need a biller?
- How many sliding-scale options should you have?
- What will your cancellation policy be?
- What information do you want to post about yourself on your website?
- Which additional training should you seek?

Some choices within this layer might feel straightforward; others feel delicate and complicated. Moreover, even a settled choice may become challenged by a personal circumstance or a client's specific needs. If you seek feedback from others about what to do, you will also receive different answers, and this can magnify decision fatigue.

Micro Therapist Self

This layer encompasses all the choices you make in the moment-to-moment interactions with your clients. It contains immense richness, yet it also can spur a sense of feeling afraid, scattered, or completely ineffective. This is because every client experience presents countless opportunities for "how to think" and "what to do."

For example, let's say you're sitting with a client, and they tell you they feel depressed. This is relatively common. So, where do you move next? Do you ask them to articulate their specific symptoms? Do you do a formal suicide assessment? Do you offer a validating statement thanking them for their disclosure? Do you ask them to rank their depression on a scale from 1 to 10? Do you acknowledge how they looked down at the floor when they told you? Do you refer them to a psychiatrist for a medication referral?

These are just some of the many paths you could take with that client. Objectively, there is no best option. But how do you know when to pivot from one approach to another?

Moment-to-moment choices must be made throughout your sessions, including:

- What should you do if a client is experiencing a panic attack?
- How should you interpret the client's making a sarcastic remark?
- Should you self-disclose about your own experience with this topic?
- Is now the right time for you to gently interrupt a group member?
- Do you need to assess further for child abuse?
- When should you ask a client more questions about their trauma?

Typically, therapists are advised to work through the challenges of decision-making by seeking external support. Unfortunately, this can also create a conundrum. Supervision and consultation do help therapists improve their skills, but receiving multiple sources of guidance can exacerbate confusion.

Have you ever presented a case in front of a group and then received eight different answers about what to do next? *Have you tried doing the empty chair technique? Have you assessed them for self-harm? Why don't you consider bringing their mother into session? What about discussing a referral to a psychiatrist? You should think about doing EMDR. No, that client is not a good fit for*

EMDR. You should refer them to a provider with more expertise. What about simply holding space and acknowledging their emotions?

These are all meaningful options. So, how do you choose? And what if you say or do the "wrong" thing?

Some micro decisions are deliberate and planned. But many of them are spontaneous and based on what you think might be best for your client at that moment. There is an unquestionable interplay between how each layer impacts every other layer, and fatigue in one layer can spill into all the rest.

GRACEFULLY MANAGING THE OVERWHELM

Decision fatigue is a collective phenomenon that isn't unique to therapists. Everyone experiences it, from the homeowner who has to choose among hundreds of shades of white to paint their trim to the financial planner deciding which stock to buy and when to buy it.

Many executives have talked openly about the perils of decision fatigue; several have shared their attempts to mitigate choice in daily life. For example, former president Barack Obama went on record saying, "You'll see I wear only gray or blue suits. I'm trying to pare down decisions." The billionaire Warren Buffett allegedly switches among three breakfast menu items at McDonald's every morning. Marie Kondo became a household name for eliminating any object that didn't spark joy.

The immense abundance of choice isn't changing anytime soon. However, you can take some steps to minimize feeling so scattered. Here are three takeaways:

1. **Choosing to commit:** Making a deliberate decision to pursue one option over others.

2. **Accepting the possibility of regret:** Acknowledging that all choices come with risk and you may later wish you had chosen differently.

3. **Remembering it's all transient and fleeting:** Recognizing that life constantly evolves, nothing lasts forever, and detaching yourself from certain outcomes can be valuable.

In the following section, we go into greater detail about these three important aspects of decision-making.

CHOOSING TO COMMIT

Committing to something always means eliminating other options. While this is scary, it can be equally liberating. But what's the best way to narrow down all the possible choices on a given day without burning out?

First, you should identify whether you resonate with "maximizing" or "satisficing" tendencies. Herbert Simon, a Nobel Peace Prize winner and political scientist who studied decision-making, observed that people generally act as either *maximizers* or *satisficers* when they make choices.[2]

If you are a maximizer, you are invested in securing the best outcomes. You dutifully research your options and weigh all potential variables before committing to your selection. For example, let's say you want to buy a new laptop for work. You check multiple models from multiple companies. You then meticulously read online reviews and spend hours comparing and contrasting prices and features. Even after making your choice, you might still check alternative options afterward to reassure yourself that you made the best one.

If you are a satisficer, you also care about making sound decisions. However, you lack the emotional pull to make the perfect choice. If you need to buy a new laptop for work, you may simply buy the newest model of the brand you already use. Even if you believe better alternatives might exist, you feel that it isn't worth spending all that time diving into them.

Both approaches have their benefits and drawbacks. It's also possible to be a maximizer in some areas of your life and a satisficer in others. However, it's likely that maximizers exhibit higher degrees of perfectionism, depression symptoms, and anxiety. The nuance is that those traits may be what predisposes someone to maximizing tendencies.

Unfortunately, chronic maximizers seem to approach decision-making under the impression that a perfect choice inherently exists. While some choices may be more advantageous than others, objective perfection isn't real. The struggle, therefore, feels even more magnified. How do you decide when you *know* some discomfort or fear might still exist?

We postulate that maximizing therapists likely feel more overwhelmed in this work than satisficers. Why wouldn't they? In such a varied field, with such limitless options available for where to work, how to work, when to work, and whom to work with, being overwhelmed has become more of an everyday rule than the concerning exception.

It's also not as simple as saying, *Just decide something and move on!* Some choices, after all, are extremely hard. The consequences associated with making the wrong decision can feel terrifying.

As a therapist, you likely witness this brand of uncertainty in your clients every day. You sit with people as they muse about whether they should quit their job, have a child, marry that man, quit drinking, or end therapy. You validate their ambivalence and ideally help them move into making their decisions if and when they're ready to take that step.

Ultimately, committing to something in your work does mean eliminating other options. And while this can feel unnerving, it can be equally empowering. Just as executives reduce decisions in daily life, it's also important for you to consider how to eliminate excessive choices in your routine.

Each layer of decision-making presents an opportunity for more simplification and automation. Now we will focus on how you can make commitments within the following layers: personal self, macro therapist self, and micro therapist self.

PERSONAL SELF

Reducing decisions in daily life can help mitigate fatigue and streamline the need to "guess" what you will do next. This helps conserve your emotional energy for more crucial decisions and can enhance your overall well-being and sense of productivity.

- **Identify your most central values:** Identify which values are most integral to your well-being and overall life purpose. If possible, narrow your list down to your top three values. While it's unrealistic and perfectionistic to expect yourself to eliminate everything existing outside those values, reflect on how well you make decisions that best honor them.

- **Limit exposure to choices:** Consider which choices can be restricted to fewer options. For instance, capsule wardrobes, meal planning, and choosing to shop at a few designated locations are popular ways people achieve this. Even if better options exist, you reduce fatigue by immediately minimizing excessive exposure to them.

- **Use automation tools:** Explore how you can automate recurring tasks, including bill payments and weekly or monthly deliveries, to avoid needing to think about when to block out time to complete these activities.

- **Establish routines:** Develop familiar, daily routines for regular activities that you must do on an ongoing basis. Routines provide a grounding sense of structure, and they can also dramatically reduce the number of choices you have to make each day.

MACRO THERAPIST SELF

Reducing decision fatigue at work often entails implementing various strategies that help you maintain a sense of familiarity throughout your day. The following principles may need to be adjusted due to specific circumstances, but they can guide you if you're feeling especially scattered.

- **When looking for a new job, write down your nonnegotiable work boundaries:** List as many as you can recognize. If you're struggling to identify any, answering the following questions may help you narrow down some choices.

  1. Are there any populations I cannot or will not work with?
  2. How long am I willing to commute to work?

3. What is my minimum compensation requirement?
4. What supervision requirements, if any, do I have?
5. Which other benefits do I need this job to have?

- **Identify clear boundaries for how, when, and where you work:** Try to make your general work policies explicit to you, your boss and colleagues, and your clients. This can reduce the need for you to spontaneously decide how you will react to a given situation.

- **Organize all professional to-do lists by level of urgency:** This strategy involves committing to tackling the tasks on your list in order of importance, which mitigates the problem of guessing which item to do next.

- **Schedule breaks each day or week:** Be mindful that "guessing" when to take a break may result in you either *never* breaking or breaking at inopportune times. Instead, try to consider when you can buffer in brief moments for reflection, mindfulness, and reconnecting with yourself during the workday.

- **Determine your after-work parameters:** Identify what you will and will not attend to when you are not working. If you allow clients to contact you, list which boundaries you still want to implement. If you allow contact only for emergencies, know what those emergencies entail.

MICRO THERAPIST SELF

Coping with micro-therapeutic decisions is delicate. All clients are unique, so no two treatments can ever be identical. The goal here is to be practical with yourself *and* respectful of the work of therapy. You can't and shouldn't "automate" how you act with clients. At the same time, it shouldn't feel as if you're constantly scattered during sessions.

As therapists, we build uniquely attuned relationships with the people we work with. It is impossible to replicate this specific and seemingly intracellular process. We talk much more about this relationship in the next section. But for now, here are some ways to manage the overwhelmed feelings that coincide with your micro therapist self.

- **Define your professional support team:** Ideally, this team will consist of trusted mentors and colleagues you can turn to for clinical consultation. If you embrace this approach, you avoid talking to any random professional when you need feedback on a case. Instead, you consistently choose to collaborate with your vetted team to avoid the possibility of receiving too many varied responses.

- **Align with one or a few theoretical orientations:** Theory can help refine treatment focus. Instead of haphazardly grabbing an exercise from a goody bag of interventions, feeling settled into theory can help you maintain a level of consistency in how you think and act with your clients. It also reduces decision fatigue, as you're agreeing to one way of conceptualizing and intervening while also saying no to other ways of being or acting. There is a deliberate commitment about how you present and intervene.

- **Accept that you can't do or be everything for every client:** You have limitations, just as all therapists do. You will make the wrong choice with some clients. Sometimes this requires flexibility and quick pivoting. Other times, it means adopting principles from the satisficer's mindset and reminding yourself that *good enough* has to be good enough.

- **Identify your therapeutic boundaries:** You should know how long each session will last, when you will complete paperwork, and how you will respond to a client if they disclose a last-minute bombshell. This job calls for flexibility, but having a clear framework in mind (for both you and your clients) decreases the number of impromptu choices you need to make. This is an integral part of implementing logistical consistency, which we discuss in chapter 5.

- **Welcome and embrace opportunities for repair:** You will make mistakes with your clients often. Modeling the ability to genuinely apologize, take personal accountability, and strive to reconnect with a client can be one of the most impactful parts of treatment. We review this in more detail in chapter 6.

ACCEPTING THE POSSIBILITY OF REGRET

The idea of committing widens space for the fear of regret to emerge. This fear can feel more pronounced for therapists who have maximizing tendencies. What happens when you move forward with one choice and you later regret your decision?

Regret deserves to be unpacked properly. Most therapists spend a great deal of time processing shame, fear, and anger with their clients. How often do you genuinely sit with either your own regret or a client's regret? Without automatically trying to reframe it? Or dismiss its relevance? We live in a society where regret is branded as an unhelpful or even useless emotion. We're also advised that the optimal way to live is to have no regrets.

Because regret is cast as a conscious choice that you can turn on or off, you may internalize that experiencing regret somehow means you don't have enough gratitude or that you live too much in the past.

This is such faulty thinking, and to emphasize our point, we turn to Daniel Pink, author of *The Power of Regret*, who highlights that regret is an essential, adaptive emotion. He shares how regret encourages people to tap into humility and be cognizant that making mistakes is an inescapable part of being human. Better yet, when we harness regret productively, we can positively shape future behavior.

Pink's research shows that as people age, they are more likely to experience what he calls "inaction regrets" versus "action regrets" in a 2:1 ratio.[3] Inaction regrets refer to the regret of not doing something, and action regrets refer to the regret of doing something. Action regrets, in many ways, can be undone. Pink conceptualizes that people are drawn toward positively justifying even suboptimal decisions with the semi-satisfying statement "At least I." *At least I asked them out! At least I learned a lot about running a business! At least I can say I have my doctorate! At least I can say I gave it my full effort!*

Pink believes optimizing regret helps people better understand their values, learn important lessons, and move forward. We think this mentality fits well for our profession. Therapists who embrace taking risks and expanding their skills likely fare better than therapists who remain complacent in their approach. Keeping your career in motion provides a sense of vivacity. That vivacity can act as a necessary safeguard against stagnation, apathy, and burnout.

In your work as a therapist, it's crucial to remember that life does not come with a dress rehearsal. It's all happening right here and in this very moment, unfolding as you read each word in this book. If this awareness stirs a sense of existential anxiety, we encourage you to pause and note that feeling. Pay attention to it. If you can, lean into it.

Time is an irrecoverable commodity. The ending is the same for everyone. No matter how or when you get there. And if regret is inevitable, we can all learn to make room for it. Habituating to regret's presence can pave clear paths for coping with indecisiveness and living meaningfully.

Coming to terms with regret can be as important as it is uncomfortable. Regret molds who people are and who they strive to be. It showcases the bittersweet nature of life, in which sorrow happens, mistakes take place, and pain is part of the process.

Sometimes it's necessary to wonder about life's unexpected twists and missed opportunities in the same way an imaginative child contemplates which superpower they wish they possessed. At other times, we may need to spend time grieving what can never be.

We like how best-selling author Cheryl Strayed exquisitely talks about her decision to have children and the troubling ambivalence she faced about saying goodbye to another possible life: "I'll never know and neither will you, of the life you don't choose. We'll only know that whatever that sister life was, it was important and beautiful and not ours. It was the ghost ship that didn't carry us. There's nothing to do but salute it from the shore."[4]

The goal can't be to try to avoid regret altogether, because you might end up feeling stuck or paralyzed. This might look like dozens of half-hearted intentions—books that remain unread, trainings you hope you will pursue, a practice you long to open, an opportunity you wish you could seize. You may think you're waiting to feel motivated, but it may be more apt to assume you're waiting to *not* worry about regret. That becomes a waiting game that may not have an expiration date.

If you do make movements while trying to mitigate regret, those movements might feel small, rigid, or controlled. This isn't wrong, but it has its risks, and one of the risks is experiencing the very regret you're trying to avoid.

No matter what, your life's ending is prewritten. How will you move both *with* and *despite* that hard truth?

Remembering It's All Transient and Fleeting

"No man ever steps in the same river twice, for it's not the same river and he's not the same man."

—Heraclitus

Despite the affinity for holding on to systems and control, nothing in life remains static. True permanence does not exist, and all that feels dominant will evolve.

Every moment on this planet changes every client and

every therapist. Nobody is the same person they were a nanosecond ago.

Take a moment to reflect on the specific timing of a particular therapeutic relationship in your life right now. Think about a certain client and imagine how different things might have been had you met a year ago instead of today. What about five years ago? What do you do in your practice today that you didn't do then? And what will your practice look like five years from today?

Take your client's development into consideration as well. What has evolved to make them exactly who they are right now? What experiences did they accumulate that led you to meet at this particular juncture in both of your lives?

You can never step in the same river twice. Everything is constantly shifting, in both tiny and extraordinary ways. We expect that whatever mental health service feels objectively relevant today will undoubtedly evolve in the future. All we need to do is take a brief look into the history of psychiatry and psychotherapy. So many massive changes have affected the mental health landscape. The concept of blank-slate therapy, the classic hallmark of psychoanalysis, is increasingly rejected by modern therapists who value bringing their human presence into their work. Furthermore, just a few years ago, most therapists eschewed the concept of providing virtual therapy. But even after the pandemic dust settled, many of the same therapists who begrudgingly transitioned to online work closed their physical offices and continued meeting with clients virtually.

Even how we understand mental health continues to change. People once believed that those with schizophrenia were possessed by demons. And the American Psychiatric Association only removed homosexuality as a diagnosis from the DSM in 1973. We're now in an era of understanding more about the intersection of trauma and mental health. We're also brushing up against looming fears of artificial intelligence seizing the industry altogether.

How is anyone supposed to keep up?

It's naive to assume that any modern-day methods or beliefs have inherent superiority. History continues to show that trends, and even what feels like factual data, evolve.

No matter how educated you become, how you are educated will change too. Therapy trends will also evolve, as new knowledge emerges, new leaders replace their predecessors, and new practices take center stage.

To be human is to be innovative. Therapy will look radically different in twenty, fifty, and a hundred years from today.

This is true for almost any industry. Large behemoths of companies file for bankruptcy. Entire industries vanish. Nobody thinks the biggest names will fall, but even those companies are not immune to change. Only 10.4% of Fortune 500 companies have stayed in that elite group since its 1955 inception. The other 90% have either filed for bankruptcy, been acquired by or merged with other companies, or fallen from their top-ranked status.[5]

We all want to give the best treatment to our clients. A popular quotation attributed to Maya Angelou states: "Do the best you can until you know better. Then when you know better, do better." But even the definition of "better" changes with new data, people, and the evolution of life itself.

Although change feels scary, it can also be incredibly exciting. As this profession progresses, there is so much hope in the unknown. What theoretical orientations will be discovered and practiced in the next hundred years? What new course content will graduate teachers teach? How will laws and ethics change? What new medications or diagnoses will be introduced? How will technology impact how we approach our work? How will our understanding of human behavior fundamentally change? How will the next generation of therapists do better than we're doing?

Nobody can know what they don't know. However, honoring the evolution of therapy offers therapists the grace of having an open mind. We can choose to ride the tides of change together.

Takeaways for Coping When You Feel Overwhelmed by Too Many Decisions

- Give yourself permission to commit to something. Make that choice that you've been waffling on and accept that fear or uncertainty will likely be present. Experiencing those emotions doesn't mean anything is wrong. Understand that there is also a cost associated with trying to wait for emotions to vanish (or never appear at all). Practice giving your emotions space while still giving yourself the gift of choosing a path.

- Strategize ways to reduce the impact of decision fatigue in everyday life. Automate and create systems when possible. Eliminate the need to decide among limitless choices by following routines or choosing from only a small selection of options.

- In areas where you often maximize, try to practice moments of satisficing. Good enough can be good enough. Be mindful that perfectionism will likely show up when you do this, but gently affirm for yourself that perfection doesn't exist. Remind yourself of the massive costs that may coincide with maximizing tendencies.

- Some regret may be unavoidable, but regret is not a bad or scary thing you must consciously strive to avoid. Focus on what you can control or decide upon with the resources you have available to you now. Trust that your future self will be equipped to cope with regret if it arises.

- Remember that the world constantly changes. Whatever theory or intervention reigns supreme today will be obsolete in the future. This is true for how we conduct therapy, and it is true for how people live their daily lives. Try to embrace riding the tide of change and having an open mind when new information is presented to you.

- When in doubt, know that very, very few choices are permanent. Trust that you can try something without needing to commit to it for the rest of your life.

Chapter 3

What If You Don't Feel Good Enough to Be a Therapist?

W

e've talked about how the lack of sufficient training or inadequate support in the field can contribute to feeling lost as a therapist. In this chapter, we explore another aspect of your professional identity, namely, the phenomenon *But what if I'm too ___?*

Can you fill in the blank for yourself?

Maybe it sounds like *But what if I'm too messed up to be a therapist? But what if I'm too passive to be a therapist? But what if I'm too stuck in my trauma to be a therapist? But what if I'm too young to be a therapist? But what if I'm too unconventional to be a therapist? But what if I'm too stupid to be a therapist?*

We could go on. Maybe you tussle with many of these deep questions simultaneously. They often tug at the most compassionate therapist's heart. They expose some of our deepest insecurities, living in the tears that may be cried alone in your office or processed in your own therapy sessions. They're almost always asked when working with your most difficult clients.

First, we'll say this: you are good enough exactly as you are.

Undeniably. You are worthy to be in this space, and you deserve to be here and have a role in this wonderful profession. No matter where you came from or exactly where you're going, this field needs therapists with varying skill sets and strengths. Here are some insights to help you anchor your unique lived experiences and extraordinary humanness to better serve yourself and your clients.

WHAT BROUGHT YOU INTO THIS PROFESSION

You didn't stumble into becoming a therapist by chance. Depending on where you are on this journey, you may have already acquired several years of advanced education. You might have earned thousands of hours toward clinical licensure. If you have been in the profession for many years, you have participated in ongoing continuing education courses and kept your license in good standing. The career is a long and expensive journey—nobody can impulsively hop through its many logistical steps.

But at some point, you made the definitive choice to become a therapist. Maybe, like many, you felt driven to help others. The origin of this drive often starts in early life. Perhaps you entered the field because you believed you had a natural affinity for the work. Whether or not it was appropriate for them to do so, family or friends may have leaned on you for your compassion and active listening skills.

Many therapists had early experiences of trying to help others; you may have inadvertently taken on a caregiving role, only to concretize it later in your professional pursuits. It's often said that people unconsciously enter this field to heal themselves, which Carl Jung emphasized in his "wounded healer" concept.[1] Later, psychoanalyst Ronald Fairbairn mused, "I can't think what could motivate any of us to become psychotherapists, if we hadn't got problems of our own."[2]

We love Fairbairn's take. It challenges the deeply rooted misconception that therapists are somehow immune to life stressors or emotional pain. It also validates that it's perfectly fine to be motivated to do something because it's *personal* to you. It's okay if you became a therapist because you wanted to better understand yourself or the experiences you struggle with. Although some motives to enter this field aren't explicitly conscious, many people experience a gripping pull toward learning about mental health to solve their own mental health problems. This makes sense—when you're struggling, you might latch on to anything that seems like it could help stop the emotional bleeding.

Therapists also enter the profession in response to their own experiences in therapy, sometimes stemming from different roots. If you had a positive therapeutic experience—if therapy really aided your healing or growth—you may feel inclined to pass along the same gifts you received. But if you had a bad time in therapy, you may feel called to become the person you needed in your own life. You want to give to others what you know you deserved to receive. Regardless of what brought you to this work, you didn't know what it was like to be a therapist until you became a therapist. Nobody does. And now, as you reflect on the motives that incentivized you to pursue this career, you might notice various reactions emerging. We invite you to spend a moment reflecting on your younger self at the starting line of your professional journey. Consider whether any of these thoughts resonates with you:

As I look back on my initial decision to become a therapist, I can see how at the time ...

- I was hopeful.

- I was unrealistic.
- I was ambivalent.
- I was directionless.
- I was afraid.
- I was curious.
- I was eager.
- I was enchanted.
- I was misled.
- I was feeling pressured.
- I was foolish.
- I was confident about my decision.
- I was chasing a dream.

You chose to become a therapist based on some conception of what it would look like for you. But there's a good chance your current reality doesn't match that original image.

For example, maybe you pictured the cozy office with a bookshelf lined with color-coordinated psychology books and lush plants everywhere. Perhaps, in the fantasy, when you weren't saving people's lives, you thumbed through those books, meditated on your couch, and engaged in wise conversations with colleagues over coffee. And in this vision, there's a good chance that you also have your life in order, you feel a deep passion for therapy, and you enjoy your clients wholeheartedly. But can reality ever match the pictures in our imagination? Even if you do have the job you always envisioned, how being a therapist *feels* is probably different from what initially sparked your interest. And if you don't enjoy your current job, which is a common problem, the difference feels even more striking. This gap between expectations and reality can be fertile ground for professional frustration.

Wherever you are today, you have already evolved from

your initial choice to become a therapist. This can happen as early as graduate school, before you even see a client. You think you know what the job entails, and then you start learning what the nuts and bolts really are. The image continues to change as you move through various settings, supervisors, actual experiences with clients, and more. It's typical to experience some disillusionment in any job. A fantasy of a career can't fill in all the spaces of the real day-to-day experience.

For some people, remembering what led them to be a therapist acts as a gentle anchor amid their fluctuating emotions. It keeps you feeling revitalized and connected to your work. That *why* can be enough to offer perspective during the hard days. But others will realize that they need to dig in and find new reasons to keep going. Your old motives for becoming a therapist may no longer serve you, so you must draw upon new sources of inspiration.

THE GIFTS OF YOUR HUMANNESS

"Doing psychotherapy tests patient and therapist alike, asking them both to deal with fears, tensions, losses, limitations, exposure and maintaining a focus on the growing edge of development through the inevitable setbacks and disappointments. But it also provides an arena for authentic relatedness and a commitment to the collaborative work of knowing a person's internal life. The potential for understanding generated by psychotherapy is unrivaled."

—Janet Lee Bachant,
Exploring the Landscape of the Mind:
An Introduction to Psychodynamic Therapy

Who were you before you became a therapist? And who are you when you step away from clients? What is your role as a friend, spouse, parent, or adult child? What gives you personal meaning? When you experience pain, how do you cope with it?

You don't have to answer these questions, but if you do, you can quickly see the immense richness emanating from your soul. You are a therapist, *and . . .* The *and* represents every other role you embody. You bring those roles into your work, even if you don't do it consciously.

Your identity, like anyone's identity, moves and changes throughout the lifespan. You entered the field with a unique constellation of relationships and milestones, and, like many therapists, you might have a nuanced history of trauma or other mental health issues. Regardless of your age or the nature of your lived experiences, we do not doubt that you have endured adversities and felt the magnitude of your shortcomings.

When we think about harnessing humanness professionally, we turn to Dr. Marsha Linehan, the founder of dialectical behavior therapy (DBT). At seventeen years old, a tender young Marsha was hospitalized in a secluded room containing just a bed, a chair, and a barred window. At the time, she had been diagnosed with a severe case of schizophrenia, and her treatment consisted of a smattering of interventions, including psychoanalysis, electroshock treatments, and antipsychotic medications. But nothing worked, and she spent over two years locked in this facility. Her discharge summary deemed her one of the most disturbed patients in the hospital.

In 2011, in an interview with the *New York Times*, Linehan reflected on her past with this poignant quote: "I felt totally empty, like the Tin Man; I had no way to communicate what was going on, no way to understand it."[3]

Linehan spent many years feeling engulfed by the desire to die. But instead of surrendering to her own despair, she forged her path of radical acceptance, which is one of the four core tenets of DBT. Linehan began working with people like herself, including those who felt chronically suicidal, because she believed she understood their suffering on a personal level.

Linehan acknowledges that she struggled with borderline personality disorder. Her contributions to the therapy profession have helped countless clients with that diagnosis find relief from their emotional pain. Today, practitioners around the world use DBT to treat a variety of mental health issues, ranging from depression to substance use. But would this model even exist without Linehan's lived experience and courage? Probably not.

You have your own anguish. You have your own weaknesses, imperfections, uncertainties, and fears. They can be exhausting and shameful. They can call you to question every part of this career. But when harnessed, they also give you an incredible new perspective.

Research on exact mental illness rates among therapists is scant, but one study from 2011 examining 800 psychologists found that 61% of respondents experienced at least one episode of what they considered to be major depression. More than 1 in 4 disclosed feeling suicidal, and 4% reported attempting suicide.[4]

We ran our own social media poll asking therapists to indicate whether they had ever been diagnosed with a mental health condition. Nearly 5,000 therapists responded, with 63% indicating that they had received a formal diagnosis. Some 20% of respondents replied that they did not have a formal diagnosis but suspected they either currently or previously met the criteria for one. Only 17% indicated never having had a mental health condition.

No matter what you have or have not endured, your vantage point is *yours*. Ideally, it supplies you with empathy and patience to engage in this meaningful work. If you want to connect with your clients, you must also connect with what makes you human. You must understand on a personal level how demanding life can be and how vulnerable certain emotions can feel.

Your humanness enables you to see other people's pain and care for them deeply. Yes, clients often need skills and guidance. They often come to us in such desperation, and they look to us for answers and wisdom. Many want to be rescued, as they've often lived their entire lives without being able to truly rely on anyone.

In chapter 6, which focuses on what clients find impactful in therapy, you will see that they rarely cite the multistep interventions or alphabet soup of certifications attached to their therapist's name. Instead, they talk about the ineffable human moments that live in the human subtleties of held eye contact, softness, warmth, and unwavering validation. They relish genuine expressions by their therapist, like "I'm so proud of you," "I'm just so glad to see you," "I was thinking about you during the week," and "You matter to me."

Your expertise makes you a therapist. Expertise lends a hand to conceptualization and applicable skills. This can't be overstated. But your humanness makes you a safe therapist. If you are not safe, your expertise is irrelevant.

So, that's the good news. There is tremendous virtue in celebrating your humanness. What makes you human makes you meaningful!

But what happens when the very things that make you human are the things that bring you the most shame? What about those unresolved, uncomfortable insecurities like trauma, mental illness, substance abuse, financial problems, or unstable relationships in your life? The shame surrounding these experiences beats its own pulse, causing you to internally ask, *How can I help someone else when I can't help myself? What if my clients knew who I really am? Why can't I follow the advice I give my clients?*

FEELING GOOD ENOUGH AS A THERAPIST

The first step toward feeling good enough is recognizing that no therapist can escape their human-first identity.

Fortunately, most clients don't want support from a stoic robot. The entire second part of this book dives into what clients value from their therapists. As you will learn, your expertise matters, but it matters less than your capacity for building trust and cultivating authentic curiosity.

But back to you. You're trying to survive in the best ways you can, leaning on the strategies and relationships that help you feel safe.

Sometimes it's messy. Sometimes breathtakingly messy. The client-therapist relationship is real, and it is co-created. Within the context of this relationship, we offer a dynamic exchange that can't be offered in self-help books, advice columns, or other sources of one-dimensional feedback. You spend your sessions tracking your clients' moment-to-moment experiences. You strive to be present and engaged, and you respond to each client based on how they present and engage with you.

MANAGING FEELINGS OF HYPOCRISY

At this point, we need to talk about therapist hypocrisy. This is such a ubiquitous struggle in our profession. Many people feel like hypocrites when they suggest that a client try something they haven't been able to do themselves. They also sometimes feel hypocritical when they're working with clients and struggling in their own lives.

Allow us to illustrate one potential example of hypocrisy. Let's say that Sally and Jim are a middle-aged couple who have been married for a decade, and they're unhappy in their relationship. They continue arguing about the same issues, and their resentment toward each other keeps growing.

They find you, a couples therapist, and they reach out for support. But you have a secret. Despite your remarkable clinical presence, you're struggling in your marriage. Your partner has pulled away and continues to reject your bids for emotional and physical intimacy. For many months, it has made you feel desperate and ashamed. In a moment of despair, you looked elsewhere to fulfill your needs, leading to an extramarital affair and perpetual patterns of deceit in your marriage.

Your clients don't know this background. So, are you a hypocrite? If you are, do the actions you've taken in your personal life nullify your clinical capabilities? And if you're not a hypocrite, what specific choices would move you into hypocrite territory?

This situation highlights the complicated paradigm of interweaving your personal life with your professional identity. It can be hard to pinpoint what makes someone a hypocrite. Most of us want to practice what we preach. It's just not always that simple or even feasible.

And, more importantly, if you do feel like a hypocrite, what should you do about it? Ethically, should therapists treat clients who are struggling with issues that closely parallel the therapists' own unresolved difficulties? This gets tricky in actual practice. Take the clinician who treats depression but privately battles with suicidal ideation. Or the therapist who

WHAT IF YOU DON'T FEEL GOOD ENOUGH TO BE A THE...   55

teaches parenting classes but snaps at her daughter in a fleeting fit of frustration. What about the trauma specialist who drinks more than she should to cope with the remnants of her past?

Are these professionals hypocrites? And if so, what is the tipping point between being an imperfect human and being unfit for this line of work?

The truth is that nobody can escape their humanness. To feel grounded in this work, it's important to understand and reconcile hypocrisy when it arises.

Reframing a Therapist's Hypocrisy

Unfortunately, when a therapist struggles with their own needs or coping behaviors, the loud inner dialogue can sound like this: *Should I even be a therapist? If my clients knew who I am or how I cope, they would be horrified. Maybe I shouldn't be doing this work. Am I a bad therapist because I'm struggling with the same thing my clients are struggling with? I should know better. I do know better!*

The concept of hypocrisy deserves to be unpacked. In a simple definition, a hypocrite is someone who acts in ways that oppose their stated beliefs. People loathe hypocrisy because it coincides with a sense of betrayal. Nobody likes feeling duped. It's threatening to trust someone who portrays themselves inaccurately.

But what *is* an accurate portrayal? To be human is to do human things, and this comprises a wide range of behaviors. It includes relapses, regressions, and regrets. It encompasses all those moments of weakness and suffering. No matter how a therapist presents themselves professionally, their personal life is not immune from these textured experiences.

Being a therapist doesn't mean you get to have it all figured out. Complete self-actualization can't be achieved in this lifetime. There is no final destination where healing or growth ends. This applies to you as much as it applies to your clients.

Of course, you care about the integrity of your work. You also logically know you can't be perfect. But how high are the standards you have for yourself? We know many therapists who wish to be fully cured or healed from whatever distress impacts them in their personal lives. They long for that, and they still want to be relatable to their clients!

If we go back to you being a couples therapist who is having an affair, is it fair to call you a hypocrite? If your clinical strategies genuinely help your clients, do your struggles invalidate your credibility?

The goal isn't to answer these questions objectively. Instead, the goal is to understand that everyone struggles and makes mistakes. And just as you wouldn't shame a client for struggling, we urge you to practice holding some of that same compassion for yourself. You are a human trying to figure it out with the resources and strategies available to you. Yes, it may feel hypocritical to engage in unwanted behaviors. But it's delusional to expect that you can act perfectly or congruently in all situations.

Reconciling hypocrisy begins with wholeheartedly accepting your limitations. Setbacks happen; mental health ebbs and flows; like everyone else, you move through your constellation of intense emotions, including guilt, sadness, fear, and disgust.

This is wonderful. It gives you perspective when you sit with clients who also feel like hypocrites, who know what to do in a given situation but struggle to implement that insight. It also gives you empathy for how hard change really is. This is the essence of humanity, and tapping into that essence brings authenticity to this work.

Finally, feeling like a hypocrite can be a necessary call to action. Consider leaning into what this feeling is trying to tell you. Maybe it's time to face some problems you've been avoiding. Maybe you should consider adopting some of the strategies you eagerly share with your clients. And maybe, when you still find it hard to change—as many people do—you choose to remain patient and kind to yourself the way you would to anyone else.

IDENTIFYING AND HARNESSING PERFECTIONISM

"Imperfection is not our personal problem—it is a natural part of existing."

—Tara Brach,
Radical Acceptance:
Embracing Your Life with the Heart of a Buddha

Therapists who don't feel "good enough" may struggle with persistent themes of perfectionism. Perfectionism doesn't make its initial appearance in a professional setting—it's often a default mode that was shaped and reinforced as early as young childhood.

The refreshing news is that perfectionistic therapists have many gifts to offer our profession. If you identify as perfectionistic, you have an intense and persistent desire to provide high-quality work. You notably care about your clients' well-being, and you take your career seriously. Your internal pressure to succeed can be quite adaptive; it may drive you to help clients in transformational ways. Such transformation could yield compounding benefits that last a lifetime. We honor that strength, but we also honor its costs.

In chapter 1, we presented our findings on the infrastructural problems affecting our profession. Far too many therapists feel untrained and unequipped to treat their clients. They are doing their best, but they may lack objective templates to measure their efficacy. If you're only comparing yourself with renowned experts—or the therapist who seems like they "have it all together"—you hold the ultimate recipe for feeling inadequate.

And yet, you still need to meet with your clients. You may be meeting with a client in a few minutes, a few hours, or just after this semester ends. The timing is irrelevant—what matters is that you will be meeting and treating people even when you haven't arrived at your utopian view of competence. This is why believing in yourself and your work is so important, whether it's your first or ten thousandth session.

How Your Perfectionism Shows Up

People are quick to label comparison as the thief of joy, but nobody can truly escape this powerful force. We are social creatures—we are wired to evaluate and measure ourselves vis-à-vis other people. That tendency is rooted in our desire to survive.

Perfectionists are more prone to upward social comparison, which refers to measuring yourself against people with attributes or abilities you deem to be superior to yours. For example, a new therapist struggling with perfectionistic tendencies may not compare themselves with other therapists exhibiting similar skill levels. Instead, they might compare their work with that of therapists who have ten or twenty years more experience.

In psychotherapist Katherine Morgan Schafler's book *The Perfectionist's Guide to Losing Control*, she states that perfectionism comes in five types: intense, classic, Parisian, messy, and procrastinator.[5] Below, we focus on how these types can show up for therapists.

> **Intense perfectionistic therapist:** The intense perfectionist strives for success at all times. You are persistent in achieving your goals, even if doing so comes at the expense of your comfort or the comfort of others. You may be a skilled therapist, and you climb and stretch yourself to new limits every time you reach a milestone. However, it feels impossible to savor your triumphs. Instead, just a moment after achieving success, you simply adjust the bar. Your grind is persistent—the hunger for pursuing bigger and greater professional accomplishments can feel relentless. If you make a mistake with one of your clients, you may berate yourself, and you might also get upset with them.

> **Classic perfectionistic therapist:** The classic perfectionist is efficient, organized, and downright reliable. Your employer and clients can depend on your steadfast predictability. The problem is that you may find yourself becoming rigid or anxious in your work. There can be an ineffable desire for therapeutic treatment to follow a predetermined agenda. Unfortunately, because therapy doesn't always go according to plan, you may have trouble being flexible and spontaneous with your clients.

> **Parisian perfectionistic therapist:** Parisian perfectionists care about being *perfectly* liked. Your greatest fear is rejection, often resulting in you compromising your own needs to placate others. Concern about hurting clients or being negatively perceived by colleagues may preoccupy your

clinical work. In sessions, you may frequently find yourself avoiding boundaries, conflict, or any sense of confrontation.

Messy perfectionistic therapist: Messy perfectionists have no problem diving into their work headfirst. Unfortunately, you struggle to finish what you start. You may adore the euphoria of a new beginning, but you lose your gusto once that initial momentum wanes. This can result in many professional false starts and unfinished projects. You may feel like you're stagnant, but the discomfort of pushing through —or the fear of making a poor decision—maintains this stuckness.

Procrastinator perfectionistic therapist: This type of perfectionist tends to be the most overlooked, and it's often because they're misunderstood as being lazy or unfocused. You might constantly fall behind on paperwork or spend months waiting to submit your hours to the licensing board. Even if you feel motivated to take action, the process of getting started can feel so daunting that you put it off. You're always waiting for the "right time," but it can feel as if the right time never comes.

Schafler notes that these categories are not fixed and that it's possible to experience perfectionism at work differently than at home or in other domains. For example, a therapist might be more of a classic perfectionist with clients but a messy perfectionist in their personal life.

In many ways, this profession shapes and reinforces perfectionism. Any reputable profession demands a rigorous level of care. The business of mental health treatment deals directly with human lives. It doesn't get more serious than that. Your clients may come to you in frenzied and grim states.

They depend on you for competent, compassionate care. Careless mistakes can result in dire consequences.

If you fail to thoroughly assess a client, you risk making a detrimental diagnostic error. If your paperwork is insufficient, the insurance company might deny coverage for necessary services. Accidentally breaching your client's confidentiality is illegal, and it could shatter your client's trust.

We don't present these examples to scare you. We trust you already know them, and that they already evoke a sense of dread. In this work, we're required to mitigate the risk of making certain errors. This sets the foundation for every licensing board's laws and ethics. On a practical level, no provider wants to face a lawsuit or lose their license. On a relational level, nobody wants to harm their client.

One of the most functional parts of perfectionism is that it is a form of anxiety. Anxiety always contains some kernels of potential truth. The worst, inconceivable event could happen. Bad things happen all the time and often without warning. Perfectionism provides a semblance of control in a world that can feel so random and haphazard. While this desire for control may not be explicit, if translated it might sound like this: *If I am a good and perfect therapist, then I am a good and perfect human, and nobody and nothing can hurt me.*

This fallacy, of course, comes at an extraordinary cost. No matter how much we try to accumulate enough mastery, success, or likability, we can't entirely block out rejection and shame. But when they do arise, we're often quick to say, *Ah, it's because I messed this thing up! If only I had done it that way!*

Perfection doesn't exist. You know this, but it's still worth emphasizing.

If we assigned ten random clients to work with a highly skilled therapist, it's unlikely this therapist would match well with each person. Imagining a perfect therapist is like imagining a perfect romantic partner. While certain traits (fidelity, kindness, sense of humor, respect) may be more universally desired than others, what feels ideal to one person may feel intolerable to someone else. It doesn't matter how good you look on paper. It matters how a client feels when they're with you, and you won't be the right fit for every person. A quirk that one client finds endearing can be offensive to another. Your approach may be validating for one person but woefully ineffective for the next.

And, believe it or not, many clients benefit from occasionally witnessing their therapist's imperfections. It can be powerfully healing for clients to recognize that their therapist has complex emotions, weaknesses, and the capacity to make mistakes, just like them. In chapter 7, we illustrate the extraordinary power of an effective rupture-repair cycle, that is, when there is a disconnect on the part of the therapist and then a subsequent reconnection, which has *everything* to do with a therapist being imperfect.

Permission to be imperfect does not mean you bring every shade of your humanness into your work. It does not mean you should condone clinical sloppiness or carelessness. Untangling from perfectionism isn't about eliminating your professionalism. Instead, it's about gently and slowly releasing the internalized pressure to embody an ideal that doesn't exist.

We all make mistakes. We're all human, with expansive ranges of emotions. We all have countertransference, physical sensations, past experiences, inner strengths, and inherent biases. You can and should take steps to recognize how each of these aspects of yourself affects your clinical work, but you can't erase their existence.

OWNING YOUR PERFECTIONISM

Perfectionism doesn't need to be conquered or overcome. You don't need to "recover" from your perfectionism. It can be one of the greatest assets to your work and your life. Why would we ever want to extinguish the part of you that likely helped you survive tenuous situations or receive meaningful recognition from others?

The paradox is that there is no perfect way to manage perfectionism.

Instead of aiming to subtract perfectionism from your life, consider what you can add to your personality profile. We like the gentle protocols that Dr. Kristin Neff,[6] the pioneer in developing and studying the concept of self-compassion, offers. Neff suggests that people turn to self-kindness when they encounter difficult moments. As we've seen, most perfectionists default to self-loathing after making mistakes. Self-kindness gives us grace for being beautifully human.

Self-kindness entails:

- Being gentle with yourself when facing challenging moments
- Being mindful of the inner critic and trying to implement more warmth and nurturance
- Trying to treat yourself the way you would aim to treat a loved one

Choosing self-kindness means being mindful of your internal judgments. It also means, at times, engaging in neutrality and externalization. You can find space to breathe when you say, *This mistake happened and I feel upset about it*, instead of saying, *I'm a failure because this mistake happened*.

This doesn't invalidate your feelings, but it does put the experience into a more realistic context.

Neff also encourages people to lean on the concept of common humanity to augment self-kindness. Common humanity refers to the universal experience of humans enduring pain or suffering. No matter how lonely you feel, you are not alone in having imperfections and struggles. While every hardship is unique, anyone who breathes suffers.

Embracing common humanity helps you move away from self-pity, which screams *poor me*, and allows you to remember that pain is a collective part of what it means to be alive. Regardless of how people present themselves to the outside world, nobody leaves this planet completely unscathed. As therapists, we know this reality quite well.

Giving yourself internal kindness is a soft journey without a concrete timeline. You can be curious and loving toward your perfectionism. Consider whether your harshest perfectionistic scripts resemble someone else's voice. They often do. Note what it feels like when you believe that voice. Then pay attention to what it feels like when you gently challenge or even disregard that voice.

Perfectionists can also benefit from intentionally *adding* mild or moderate discomfort in their daily lives. This idea parallels the techniques of exposure therapy. You embrace being an amateur at something new and practice tolerating the sting associated with making mistakes or looking silly. Consider the scenario of trying a new hobby for the first time. A novice might display some natural talent, but they will naturally look clumsy next to the expert. Nobody can start as an expert, and there can be tremendous delight in enjoying an activity without needing to be the best at it.

Try adding a growth-oriented approach to your work. This can soften the need to "know it all" or "have it all figured out."

It feels empowering to take on a mindset of perpetual learning, and it can shift you away from *I should have done better* into *What can I take away from this experience? What did I learn? What can I do differently next time?*

These tasks are easier said than done. Instead of calling it a "work in progress," we think it's more fitting to call this shift a "love in progress." You're practicing loving yourself, and someone who truly and wholeheartedly loves themselves can own their perfectionistic tendencies and work within those constraints with flexibility and tenderness.

We both struggle with perfectionism in various parts of our lives. It shows up in our clinical work, and it certainly has accompanied us throughout the drafting, editing, and publishing of this book. Have we written about perfectionism as perfectly as we could have? Have we chosen the most perfect words to describe how perfectionism feels? Have we perfectly presented how readers can cope with their perfectionism?

Of course not. How could we? How could anyone?

The last part of owning perfectionism is *moving through*. For example, even though this section isn't written perfectly, because it can't be, we have to move through. We have to accept that it may still feel incomplete or even a bit unsatisfactory. We have to trust that it's still worth putting out into the world. Perfection is a mirage. If we had waited until every word felt flawless, this book never would have been published.

Owning your perfectionism is part of owning your authenticity. And when you own your authenticity, you lean into living a more meaningful life. This benefits you, and it benefits your clients. It is wonderful to be imperfect, and it is amazing to be different. Most mistakes can be altered or revisited. And even when they can't, growth can still be achieved.

You need to hold yourself to a professional standard of excellence. But excellence is not the same as perfection. An excellent therapist recognizes their weaknesses and deficits and manages them accordingly.

Finally, even if perfectionism were truly attainable in this lifetime, we don't believe it would be a worthy trait for therapists. Would you want to work with someone completely unaffected by life's adversity? Would you feel comfortable opening up to a provider who had no personal experience with failure, loss, or regret? One who didn't occasionally mess up? We know we wouldn't.

Gentle Reminders When You Don't Feel Good Enough

- Remember that nobody can escape their human-first identity. The good news is that most clients benefit from your humanness. It's what makes for an authentic therapeutic experience.

- Accept that you will never have it all figured out. This does not make you a hypocrite or a fraud. It makes you a human. Leaning into this can help you harness greater compassion and empathy for your clients who are also trying to figure things out.

- If a sense of hypocrisy keeps knocking at you, reflect on what you might be avoiding doing for yourself (that you frequently recommend clients do). Consider any small or large steps you can take to tackle this avoidance. If you can't take those steps today, see if you can lean into some self-kindness while you wait.

- Honor the fact that perfectionism is often a form of ensuring an important sense of control. It's rooted in survival and self-protection. With that, remember that nobody can be a perfect therapist. You don't have to stop being a perfectionist, but practicing self-compassion helps soothe some of the painful sharpness.

- Trust that you're a harsher critic of yourself than anyone else is. And if you have critics in your life who are harsher than you, it may be worth reevaluating your relationships!

CHAPTER 4

How Do You Strengthen Your Competence?

We have highlighted some reasons why therapists often feel incompetent in their work. Some of the problems represent internal dilemmas: you might be managing perfectionistic tendencies, coping with personal adversity, navigating decision fatigue, or just not feeling good enough in this role. Other issues are more systemic: you didn't receive adequate training, you've been assigned clients with symptoms that you have not been trained to treat, you don't feel knowledgeable in treating them, and your supervisor is nowhere to be found.

In part II, using the CHAIR model, we will share what clients find most beneficial in therapy. Strengthening those skills can augment your career at any stage. Through embodying CHAIR, you gracefully remember that *your presence* is an intervention, and sometimes it's the most important intervention you can offer a client.

At the same time, building concrete competence also matters in this work. You want to be able to examine your skills and determine how you progress within this career. In this section, we provide some practical strategies for becoming a more effective therapist—no matter what stage you've reached in your clinical practice.

In 1974, psychologist David Ricks introduced the concept of *supershrinks*, which refers to a small sample of highly effective therapists.[1] He studied the outcomes of a group of adolescents receiving therapy and discovered that one particular group of adolescents, treated by one specific therapist, consistently fared better in adulthood. His research has since been expanded by Scott Miller, founder of the International Center for Clinical Excellence. Miller has found that clients working with supershrinks are 50% less likely to drop out of therapy prematurely. These clients also improve by at least 50%. In addition, the top 20% of therapists consistently outperform the other 80% of therapists combined.[2]

These are some dizzying statistics, and, as we mentioned in our introduction, they are hardly comprehensive. Even if only some therapists are at the absolute top of their game, the American Psychological Association also reports that approximately 75% of clients benefit from therapy.[3]

Statistically speaking, you're helping your clients, even if you're average at what you do. And even if you feel woefully insecure, you're probably facilitating some successful therapeutic outcomes.

But if you want to build competence, here are some guidelines to consider.

DELIBERATE PRACTICE

In 2008, Malcolm Gladwell sensationalized the concept of 10,000 hours in his best-selling book *Outliers*. He demonstrated how people could become experts in anything from software development to music after 10,000 hours of practicing the skill.[4]

What if we applied that round number to our field? Let's say you meet with twenty-five clients a week, and you work fifty weeks a year. This equates to 1,250 hours of therapy sessions annually. If you loosely follow Gladwell's math and maintain this pace, you could theoretically become an expert in eight years. And if you see thirty clients a week, that time span moves down to about six and a half years.

Gladwell's 10,000-hour theory was inspired by a lesser-known psychologist, Anders Ericsson. Ericsson, who was once deemed "the experts on experts," spent nearly twenty years studying the world's best mathematicians, violinists, chess players, pilots, and others.[5]

Gladwell and Ericsson both vehemently believed that experts were made instead of born. But Ericsson's studies also show that superior performance emerges from a steady diet of grit and perseverance. Experts don't just practice for the sake of practicing. They deliberately practice with a supreme dedication to their craft.

This means that more hours sitting in the therapy chair doesn't correlate with having more expertise. In fact, in January 2024, psychologist Terrence Tracey and colleagues commented on therapist efficacy by stating, "The literature is clear in demonstrating that therapists do not get better over time in their ability to effect client change."[6] Similar results have been demonstrated many times.

Psychologist Scott Miller's work also supports this theory. His research shows that experienced therapists are not necessarily producing better results than graduate students are. Many providers plateau early in their careers, and their competence can decrease over time.[7]

What is happening here? First, it's well known that newer

therapists receive the most oversight in their work. Ongoing monitoring may prime them to be more reflective and analytical. If you're regularly receiving supervision, you're being exposed to how other therapists think and intervene. This may encourage you to be more reflective when meeting with clients.

In addition, when you're new to something, you may be more vigilant in how you practice. For instance, a new therapist may spend far more time conducting a thorough intake. An experienced therapist, on the other hand, may rush through it, assuming they already know some of the answers. A therapist in training might take the time to deeply understand a client's presenting issue. Someone more seasoned might just automatically fill in the blanks based on how other clients have presented in the past.

It's easy to spend years chipping away at a skill without improving that skill. Someone can spend decades cooking chicken without cooking it well. Making chicken a hundred times doesn't make you skilled at cooking chicken. If you're a fantastic chef, you might subscribe to the idea that cooking is an art. We would agree. But we also know that all art entails drawing upon specific and proven techniques. Your artistry doesn't matter if the chicken is undercooked.

When it comes to therapy, Jon Frederickson, another pioneer in the field, offers some key takeaways. Frederickson is a therapist, author, and founder of Intensive Short-Term Dynamic Psychotherapy (ISTDP). But before he moved into those roles, he was a professional musician. As any musician knows, expertise comes down to thousands of hours engaging in rote, mechanical practice. Music, like cooking, is also considered an art. But the art still requires skill and mastery. Just as nobody wants to eat undercooked chicken (even if it's made artistically!), few people would willingly attend a concert of musicians playing instruments haphazardly. The pleasure we all glean from awe-inspiring art lies at the intersection of how the artist creatively applies technical skills.[8]

When Frederickson began studying therapy, he was surprised by the lack of attention focused on building mastery. In addition to being a musician, he was also the child of a blacksmith. In both disciplines, there is a clear emphasis on structure and precision. Frederickson's contributions to the therapy profession have largely focused on the idea of *deliberate practice*, which refers to intentionally practicing specific skills at your current level of development.

So, achieving competence in our field isn't about clocking 10,000 hours. Innate talent may play a role, but research shows that one of the clearest divergences between average providers and supershrinks is the amount of time spent *deliberately* practicing therapy. We like how psychologist Daryl Chow states it: "Clinical practice is what you do in-sessions; deliberate practice is what you do before-and-after sessions."[9]

Guidelines for Deliberate Practice

Lean into the concept of therapy as a craft: Crafts require specific skills coupled with the knowledge to apply those skills. Regardless of your theoretical orientation, the main ingredients of therapy will always include some variations of empathy, active listening, effective communication, and the ability to help solve problems.

Identify your greatest clinical weaknesses: When do you find yourself stumbling in your work? What causes clients to prematurely terminate with you? Where do you feel most insecure? After listing your top three weaknesses, write down exactly what you need to do to start working on those weaknesses.

Be intentional: Before each session with a client, ask yourself, *What skill do I want to practice today?* Make it explicit (ending the session on time, setting a boundary about payment, allowing for silences, assigning homework) and, after the session, rank how well you did and specify any obstacles you experienced. If you did not practice the skill, indicate what prevented you from doing so. Track your patterns and review them with a supervisor or consultation group.

Work with a skilled supervisor: Like a coach, this supervisor should also be able to pinpoint where you can improve *and* should actively support you in strengthening those skills. This helps create a road map for applying clinical conceptualizations in actual practice. If you don't have this kind of supervisor available to you, it may be worth finding one. If money is a concern, keep in mind that many supervisors offer a sliding scale or will work with you on your budget. If this option remains beyond your budget, look for a free or low-cost consultation group or form a peer consultation group in person or online. At a very minimum, it's important to have a trusted person who can give you feedback regularly.

Watch as much therapy footage as you can: Experimenting without a road map is not always the preferred way to practice a skill. We all need to watch and observe others to gain insight into how we can apply such techniques. Just as you watch video tutorials to learn other skills, consider applying this strategy to your clinical work.

You can access many free videos on YouTube as a starting point.

Seek training opportunities that emphasize feedback-oriented practice: Skillfully applying certain models or interventions entails an extraordinary amount of practice. Unfortunately, many trainings use traditional lecture style or asynchronous learning formats. Look for trainings where you can practice skills in real time while receiving feedback from competent trainers.

Rely on self-reporting protocols if all else fails: After your sessions, assess exactly what went well and identify one mistake you believe you made. Think about what you would have done or said differently. The goal is not to ruminate or berate yourself; the goal is to build a habit of simply reviewing your performance to assess where you next need to focus your efforts.

Don't assume you need to be a supershrink to be a good therapist: Perfectionism is a professional peril. You do not need to become the top therapist in the world. People often demonize the notion of being average, but *average* therapists still tend to perform excellent work. Regardless of your current skill level, it's also helpful to have blueprints for building effectiveness and feeling more competent in your work.

Seek Consistent Feedback

Supershrinks are effective, yes, but Miller's research shows that they tend to receive more negative feedback from clients in the early stages of therapy.[10]

This may seem surprising. You would think top therapists would earn glowing recognition at all points of treatment. You would also think clients would believe they were working with the best of the best right from their first session.

In actuality, it's more complicated. Miller has an intriguing take: he suggests that supershrinks are simply more adamant and persuasive in obtaining feedback from their clients. Due to their excellent interpersonal skills, they may just make it safer for clients to vocalize concerns within the course of therapy. Therefore, they have plenty of opportunity to repair misattunements and mistakes swiftly.

So, what happens when a client provides negative feedback? A supershrink can use this evaluation to immediately address the problem. They also now have guidance for reorienting their treatment to better suit the client's needs. This is attunement in action, and their receptiveness shows clients that feedback is both safe and welcome.

Receiving negative feedback as a motivator tends to be a consistent theme among all experts. We have all heard those clichéd stories of famous actors or authors being told they would never amount to anything. Many highly successful people speak openly about their failures, sharing how others discounted their work or criticized their vision.

Some supershrinks disregard negative feedback and stay on their path, succeeding nevertheless. Others pay attention to the remarks and integrate them to improve their craft. As a therapist, it's important to balance both responses. If you hyperfocus on every single piece of negative feedback, you risk losing the essence of your work. But if you disregard something critical, you equally miss a pivotal opportunity to grow and improve.

So-called average therapists also receive negative feedback.

But if you receive that feedback too late—such as when a significant rupture occurs or after a client has already chosen to end therapy—repair may be much more challenging, if it's possible at all.

Many therapists fear receiving feedback from their clients. It's easy to confuse feedback with criticism, and it's also easy to assume criticism is a direct attack on your competence or effectiveness. If you already struggle with feeling inept with your clients, worrying about whether they feel the same about you feels especially intimidating.

You might try to mitigate this anxiety by unconsciously avoiding seeking feedback. Maybe you chug along with your clients and hope what you're doing is working well enough. You may hesitate when it comes to doing deeper self-reflective work. Confronting perceived flaws can certainly feel threatening. And if others comment negatively about your work, you may find that you quickly spiral into feeling ashamed, defensive, combative, or shut down. Any of these responses can hinder your growth and perpetuate low self-esteem.

Negative feedback can be tough to reconcile, and ultimately you can't be the right therapist for every client. But while it's impossible to please every client, it is crucial to identify shortcomings and weaknesses. Knowing what isn't working can help you focus on what needs to change. Taking feedback—and taking it well—is undoubtedly a part of this job.

Guidelines for Seeking Feedback

Seek feedback from clients: Collaborate with clients by asking them how they feel about their treatment progress so far. Learn what they are taking away from sessions or what they thought about during the week. Be receptive to any fears or concerns they present to you. It's helpful to know what is and isn't working. If something isn't working, discuss what needs to change.

Prioritize creating a feedback-oriented culture in your practice: This means both implicitly and explicitly conveying how much you want to make sure your clients are getting what they need from you. Emphasize that you might make mistakes, but that you are dedicated to addressing those mistakes if and when they occur. Be mindful that clients may indicate that all is well, even when it's not. It can be helpful to check in routinely with questions like "Is there anything else I should know?" or "What haven't we talked about that's important to you?" If you note a significant gap between their targeted treatment goal and the progress they're making toward it, this could indicate that things aren't going as well as they'd like.

Present your struggles to a supervisor or in consultation: Seek feedback from other professionals. If you feel stuck with a client, ask for help and brainstorm together. After you try those suggestions, review how well it went and what might need to be modified moving forward.

Note trends that speak to your work: What keeps certain clients coming back to you? If everyone on your caseload had to describe your strengths and weaknesses, would their responses be similar or dramatically different? Why do you think that is?

So, to review, we believe insecurity and uncertainty are ubiquitous emotions for therapists. We imagine that almost everyone in this field can relate to feeling overwhelmed, imperfect, or simply not enough. These struggles, while challenging, do not necessarily indicate that you are doing something wrong. Instead, they epitomize what it means to be a human who is offering meaningful relational experiences for clients.

You won't ever be perfect. However, you can practice self-compassion and more inner acceptance. You can also commit to building more professional competence. In part II, we will discuss these aspects of your professional identity in more depth, prioritizing strategies for gaining greater acceptance of who you are as well as meeting your goal of providing excellent service to your clients.

PART II

DEEPENING YOUR JOY AND MEANING WITH CLIENTS

Chapter 5

What Do Clients Value Most from Therapy?

"When you expect nothing from the world—not the light of the sun, the wet of water, nor the air to breathe—everything is a wonder and every moment a gift."

—Michael Sullivan, *Percepliquis*

Introduction to CHAIR

In part I, we highlighted the insecurities and difficulties therapists encounter in their daily work. We believe this validation is paramount, as many therapists worry that questioning their careers means something is fundamentally wrong with them.

Nothing is wrong with you. The job is hard, the stakes are high, and you care deeply about the welfare of your clients.

Furthermore, in therapy, just as in life, there is so much you can't control. This section focuses on what you *can* control. Right here, right now, and directly from your therapist chair. This is why the title of our framework feels so fitting: It's called

CHAIR. CHAIR stands for consistency, hope, attunement, impact, and repair.

Consistency: Maintaining a predictable and beneficial sense of stability

Hope: Holding on to and harnessing hope, even when the situation feels most dire

Attunement: Accurately interpreting and responding to your client's needs

Impact: Heightening emotion, delivering insight, and facilitating change for your clients

Repair: Recognizing mistakes and attending to ruptures within the therapeutic relationship

The chapters in part II are devoted to deeply understanding and applying practical techniques within the CHAIR framework. In this chapter, we talk about exuding a consistent presence, instilling hope, and attuning to your clients. Chapter 6 focuses on initiating therapeutic impact, which refers to how you can intentionally strive to change how your clients think or respond to a situation. Chapter 7 offers an overview of what to do when you make a mistake or upset a client.

These are not original concepts. We have practiced them informally throughout our careers, although we didn't have a specific concept that fully synthesized them. The CHAIR framework was inspired by a viral social media post in 2022. On Instagram, Nicole posed a community question to her followers: *What was the most defining moment of your therapy treatment?* She received 19,000 responses and separated them into the five categories that compose CHAIR.

In your practice, we hope you get feedback from your clients about what's working well. Maybe you're a client in therapy yourself, so you know what benefits you. But how often do you have access to 19,000 clients sharing their insights about what defined their therapy?

Here, of course, is where disclaimers matter. Social media is not evidence-based or factual. We did not attempt to verify the respondents' identities, meaning some people may not have answered honestly or been actual clients of therapy. But nuance applies in all research, and no study is flawless.

In this book, we focus on chronicling real therapists working in real-time situations with real clients. The realness can't be overstated, even if it's not captured in research sample sizes or graduate school textbooks. And many of those therapists and clients are on social media, scrolling and liking and hoping to glean insights about this profession. They're people like us, and they might be people like you.

We do trust the essence of these 19,000 responses. Fortunately, many studies corroborate our findings, and we cite some of those studies throughout this section.

CHAIR speaks to what benefits clients in therapy. Some findings may surprise you. Others will feel reassuring and grounding. As you will learn, the impact of therapy rarely comes from having advanced expertise or from executing complex, multistep interventions. Instead, therapeutic efficacy often coincides with your courage to sit with another human as openly and compassionately as possible. It also coincides with your ability to prioritize safety at all points of treatment.

The good news is that our framework can be applied at every stage of your career. It surpasses clinical theory, population, and years of experience working. You don't need any additional training to practice these skills—you can start trying them right now.

The skills are interconnected, hinging on one another, and should all be equally prioritized as you conceptualize your therapy treatment. While the framework does not fully apply to every client or clinical situation, we believe having a working knowledge of CHAIR can support therapists throughout their work.

Your presence is an intervention. The relationship can be a catalyst for change.

CONSISTENCY IN YOUR CLINICAL PRACTICE

What's impactful is that she's completely there. Week after week. She always has my favorite blanket folded up on the couch for me. And she has several blankets in her office, but she remembers which one is mine. It is consistent, and it is safe.

He consistently tells me, "That wasn't your fault."

She holds the boundaries. I don't always like that, but she always holds them. So I know I can trust her and trust this.

These are just some of the many answers we received demonstrating the importance of consistency within therapy. When you are consistent, you exude a sense of reliability and predictability. This, in turn, can foster trustworthiness. Trustworthiness is, of course, the main underpinning of any successful relationship.

Trust develops over time. Clients need to *trust* that you are safe. Providing a familiar and steady environment—with your client's best interests at heart—forms the building blocks of trust in the therapeutic relationship. Think about attachment theory, which is largely rooted in the premise of positive consistency. Babies come into this world completely helpless. They depend on a predictable sense of safe love modeled to them. If their caregivers accurately respond to their needs, babies are likely to develop strong self-esteem and resilience. When a child's needs are valued, the child learns to trust both themselves and the world around them. This creates a foundation for a secure attachment style.

Your clients are certainly not helpless infants. But many of them enter therapy after years of being hurt by people who were supposed to be safe.

UNDERSTANDING THE THREATS OF INCONSISTENCY

Babies thrive when they have attuned caregivers who can appropriately respond to their needs. However, some caregivers are inconsistent in their reactions. Sometimes, they react to their child with gentle love. But at other times, they act defensively or with hostility.

If a caregiver acts unpredictably, children often grow up feeling unsafe and uncertain. Like playing a slot machine in a casino, a child in this type of home feels as if winning is "random" and can't be expected. But they will still try to get their needs met, often developing hypervigilance to try to secure their caregiver's love.

Inconsistency erodes trust. Here's a mundane example to illustrate this point: Would you want to dine at a restaurant where the food tasted delicious only 65% of the time? We wouldn't. You might even opt to eat somewhere that is consistently average instead of gambling on the possibility of having a fabulous meal or a terrible one. This speaks to why some people gravitate toward chain restaurants, even if the food isn't the best. People care about familiarity and convenience—they may even value it more than securing premier quality.

If you bring an inconsistent presence into the therapy room, you risk unnerving clients. Therapy is already a vulnerable experience. Your predictability creates a familiar structure, and that structure provides safety. Without safety, the work can feel too threatening.

When we talk about inconsistency, we differentiate between *logistical inconsistency* and *emotional inconsistency*. Both matter and both often interconnect. Logistical inconsistency occurs when therapists are unpredictable in their standard protocol and routine of conducting therapy. People who answered our poll shared these types of experiences. For instance, one survey respondent said, *My therapist would just cancel sessions at the last minute. A few times, she let our sessions run over by a good ten minutes, but then she cut other ones short. It seemed so random.* Someone else said, *I was told I could email them in between sessions. They responded quickly once, and then they didn't respond during an actual emergency. I felt really guilty and unsure if I did something wrong.*

As a therapist, you always have the right to change your policy or even make exceptions. But if you do, it is important to explicitly convey how and when new rules will take effect. Clients may have reactions to change, particularly if they have a history of insecure attachments or relational trauma. You owe it to your relationship to hold the container for them to express those emotions safely.

Emotional inconsistency refers to being unpredictable in your responses or affect. This could mean that you sometimes come across as warm and validating, and you sometimes come across as dismissive and bored. Like a child who can't tell what mood their caregiver is in, clients with emotionally inconsistent therapists may spend more time playing detective than freely sharing their thoughts and feelings. They might also ruminate over your reactions or intensely read into what transpired in a given session.

Because therapy is relational, we all must model consistent reactions and security for our clients. Here are some thoughts about how to do that:

MODELING POSITIVE CONSISTENCY

Ideally, a client should be able to trust implicitly that you're there for them. *Being there* means being authentically you in a consistent, predictable way. Surprises are minimal because the flow of therapy feels predictable and comforting. Your client can grow to depend on you for your familiar presence.

Therapy shouldn't feel like gambling. Even when a client feels nervous to disclose something or worried about bothering you, they should have some sense of how you might respond. It is painful for clients to hope to secure your attention or kindness. It can be crushing to feel like you can't be relied upon.

Positive consistency in therapy means providing predictable and beneficial stability over time. This consistency must be *both* logistical and emotional.

LOGISTICAL CONSISTENCY

Therapists who excel in logistical consistency convey a sense of concrete reliability in their work. If this is you, you are fairly routine-oriented: You start and end sessions on time and adhere to a predictable set of clear boundaries throughout treatment. Your consistency is pragmatic and tangible.

Everyone knows what to expect, reducing the chance of dramatic surprises within the treatment process.

Therapists with logistical consistency do what they say. If you make an exception, the exception is necessary and often made out of an obvious desire to attune to your client's needs. We will discuss this in more detail in the next section.

Logistical consistency is not the same as being overly rigid. This job often calls for flexibility, and meaningful exceptions are always possible. The difference is that *consistent* therapists have a familiar baseline. When they make exceptions, it's within the parameters of that baseline. There is also intention behind those exceptions. If asked, a consistent therapist can articulate why they're doing something differently in that moment or with that client.

Inconsistent therapists, on the other hand, may feel scattered or dysregulated when organizing their treatment protocols and practices. If they don't have a familiar routine, there's no actual space for making an exception—because nothing feels like a set routine anyway! The therapist genuinely may not know why they made a certain change, and they might also not know how it impacts their client.

Strengthening Logistical Consistency with Clients

- Transparently discuss your boundaries before and throughout the treatment process when needed. Clients should know your policies with regard to payment, scheduling, cancellations, and communication between sessions. If you make changes to these policies, share them explicitly with your clients. Clients should not have to guess what your boundaries are.

- Start and end sessions on time. If exceptions to this kind of scheduling need to be made, communicate this in advance with your clients.

- When possible, aim to create a familiar physical or virtual environment in each interaction. Be mindful of moving furniture or art around. Keep lighting the same. If you typically meet in different locations (i.e., you don't have the same office each week), clients should be aware of this, and you should be mindful that it could impact their level of comfort.

- If you choose to make therapeutic exceptions (waiving a cancellation fee, extending session time, offering to reduce a rate), articulate your clinical reasons for doing so. Understand that clients may have reactions to any exceptions. Making exceptions can certainly be the right choice, but clients should not feel like they are gambling in an attempt to win an exception.

EMOTIONAL CONSISTENCY

As mentioned, we received more than 19,000 responses to the question, *What was the most defining moment of your therapy treatment?* Thousands of those replies accentuated the importance of a therapist's ability to offer emotional consistency.

We define *emotional consistency* as your capacity to maintain a reliable emotional presence with your clients. Although this kind of consistency is somewhat subjective, it is paramount for building trust and safety. Here are some responses that capture the power of therapists exhibiting positive emotional consistency:

> *I can't think of one single defining moment. Instead, what's been most defining is her ability to always respond with care. Every single time.*

> *He's unflappable. I can tell him anything, and he never stops being warm.*

> *What's most defining is that I can practically sense how she will respond. You'd think that would get old, but it doesn't. It's like nothing fazes her, and that allows me to just be myself.*

The experience of positive consistency happens when your clients can essentially predict your demeanor. They can generally trust that you won't change regardless of what content or mood they bring into the session. When this happens, over time, clients can internalize that you really can handle their constellation of emotions and needs.

Prioritizing emotional consistency begins when therapists internally acknowledge the power differential in the therapy relationship. You may not like this differential, but it exists. Many clients come to you because they perceive you to be an expert. They invest time, money, and emotional energy into their treatment. They rely on you to create a warm and inviting atmosphere as they share some of the more shameful and scary parts of their lives. Despite any fluctuating states they may be experiencing, it is your job to hold steadiness.

Many clients have been betrayed by people they once trusted. Naturally, they come to therapy wounded and afraid. Even if they desire your help, they might feel anxious about getting hurt again.

Some clients may become angry at your efforts to care for them. They might reject your compassion if they don't believe they genuinely deserve it. Others will become overly people-pleasing, doing what they can to secure your approval. Some present as highly passive, waiting for you to lead and set the tone for their treatment. None of these responses is problematic—they speak to clients who silently wonder, *Can you handle me? Are you really here for me? Because if you're not, I'm not sure if I can do this.*

The work of therapy is so tender. Your role is to stay with clients as they experiment with their emotions and try to build a secure base with you.

How you intervene as a therapist also reinforces emotional consistency. This is why we believe adhering to one or a few specific modalities can be helpful. If conducting therapy feels like you're trying on different interventions to see what fits, clients may struggle to adapt to this variance. If, for example, you're doing a trauma narrative one week, an empty-chair exercise the next, and a meditation after that, the flow can feel unpredictable and even unsettling.

We are not saying eclectic therapy is wrong. Almost every therapist embraces some integrative approach to their work. Rigidly believing that only one method works is bound to alienate clients and limit your capacity to grow. Eclectic therapy has its place, but it can't resemble haphazardly throwing noodles on the wall to see what sticks. A client is not a lab rat in a test experiment.

If you struggle with the question of whether you are emotionally consistent, consider asking yourself, *How do I want to be with my clients?* This is much different from the question most therapists ask, which is, *What do I want to do with my clients?*

Your "be" refers to your overarching presence. It refers to

the interpersonal qualities you hope to regularly convey, and it speaks to how you want clients to feel when they're with you.

As you read through the list below, think about which two or three words best encapsulate how you want to be with your clients:

- Authentic
- Insightful
- Flexible
- Friendly
- Relatable
- Safe
- Humorous
- Spiritual
- Intelligent
- Bold
- Attentive
- Creative
- Gentle
- Patient
- Empowering
- Eccentric
- Adaptable
- Compassionate
- Empathic
- Trustworthy
- Intuitive
- Honest
- Charismatic
- Introspective
- Playful

No one quality is better than another. They are all worthwhile, and different clients benefit from different types of therapeutic presences. Your qualities may also change throughout your career. Certain niches or trainings might shape different values, and evolving your skills and techniques is a normal part of professional development. However, no therapist can carry every quality with equal weight. Trying to prioritize every quality at once puts you at risk of being "a mile wide but an inch deep."

And while there is no "right" way to be, you probably gravitate toward certain qualities from the above list more than others. You can choose what you naturally feel inclined to do. Or you can embrace taking on a mindset that you want to emulate. There is no right or wrong way to do this.

The more you can lean into *how you want to be*, the more authentic you will feel, and the more emotional consistency you will naturally exude.

Strengthening Emotional Consistency with Clients

- Ask yourself, *How do I want to be with my clients?* Think about which adjectives stand out, and note which ones feel most weighted and salient. Work within theories that honor your desired therapeutic presence.

- Be mindful of how stress from your personal life bleeds into your presence at work. Of course, you are a human and allowed to have emotions and needs. But your client relies on you for safety and consistency. Try to keep this in mind when approaching your sessions, even if you're experiencing an off day yourself.

- Avoid arbitrarily trying new interventions without considerable thought and planning. Consider using interventions from the same or similar theoretical orientations. If you are training in a new model, discuss with a supervisor how you can appropriately integrate what you're learning in ways that still honor your current treatment mode. Dramatically changing your approach can be unsettling and destabilizing for certain clients.

- Integrate feedback from clients about what is and isn't working. If something is not working, consider how you can pivot treatment accordingly. If you can't, you may need to consider providing a referral to another provider.

- Think about the most important values you strive to exhibit as a therapist. Consider when those values might be compromised and brainstorm possible solutions for how you can anchor yourself back to them.

- Identify times when you may be inconsistent with clients. Consider whether any patterns exist and then reflect on what's happening within you that could trigger inconsistent responses. Such patterns may speak to unresolved personal issues, which you may be able to address in supervision or your personal therapy.

- Strive to present yourself similarly in your professional endeavors. Like most therapists, you probably have an online presence. Be mindful that clients may look you up to learn more about you and your personal preferences or other ventures. While you are so much more than your therapist identity, consider how a client's perception of you might be affected by seeing you in your other public roles.

HOW TO HOLD ON TO HOPE

Therapists work with despair across the lifetime. You can see despair in your child clients who live in unstable, unsupportive homes. You can find it in your older clients who are grieving the loss of loved ones. Anguish exists in every age, demographic, and presenting issue. At times, the heartbreak of what it means to be alive feels downright debilitating. How do we therapists hold space when that very space feels like it's been swallowed by the world's cruelty?

If anyone has something to say about hope, it's Viktor Frankl, a leading psychotherapy pioneer and author of one of the most influential books ever written, *Man's Search for Meaning*. A Holocaust survivor, Frankl lost his mother, father, brother, and pregnant wife in Nazi concentration camps. Frankl himself spent three years enslaved in four concentration camps, including Auschwitz.

While Frankl was a brilliant psychiatrist whose work has inspired generations of people worldwide, he was not an idealist. During those three years, he survived some of the most deplorable conditions a person can endure, and his book captures the rawness of such depravity. But amidst these unimaginable traumas, Frankl argued that all life had meaning. He felt that the ability to hold on to meaning, even in dire situations, was the antidote to hopelessness. This quest toward meaning is the basic concept of what became Frankl's *logotherapy* model.

Of all the emotions a therapist can feel about therapy or toward a client, hopelessness is one of the most dangerous. Giving up on a client or the value of life altogether closes creative doors and shrinks the space for curiosity. It can compromise your capacity to truly listen and problem-solve.

If a client feels hopeless, and you feel equally hopeless with them, you might hit an impasse together. How much can you help another person when you lack hope for their situation?

The idea of *unconditionally* holding on to hope remains one of the most important ideas we want to impart here. Our profession calls for brave, wholehearted, unwavering hope. Clients will lose hope, feel scared, revert into unwanted behaviors, and worry that things can never improve. If you align with that despair, you risk halting all movement.

Textbook vignettes make change sound so dramatic. It just takes a few sessions, a couple of brilliant interventions, and the client is symptom-free and healed! But true change is often far more subtle. It's not just the isolated client reaching out to a friend. It's the isolated client starting to *think* that reaching out to a friend might be a good idea. It's not necessarily a grieving client attending a support group. It's about that client recognizing they need support in the first place.

Hopeful therapists notice these slight changes, and they maintain an attitude of hope by unconditionally respecting the client's pace of growth, "slow" as it may feel sometimes. They believe that no matter what, people can change.

Hope as a therapist also means believing, at a cellular level, that there is beauty in this lifetime. Clients who have endured the worst of tragedies can experience and should experience this beauty. Goodness exists, and being a therapist means believing in reform and transformation. Many times, even when we can't change anything, we can share our hope by deepening our connection by directly or indirectly expressing to clients, *I see your pain, I see how it affects you, and even if I can't fix it all, I will be here to support you through it.*

Below we'll share some of our favorite hope-based responses to the question, *What was the most defining moment of your therapy treatment?*

It was the moment I realized he was never going to give up. No matter how many times I relapsed. He was always going to believe I could get better.

When she told me, "It's not okay right now, and it may not be okay for a long time, but one day, you will be okay."

My therapist looked right at me and said, "I have 100% faith that you can do this."

It was when I cried for the first time in therapy. I finally felt safe enough. After feeling like therapy wasn't working for me because I couldn't open up, I felt hopeful I was on the right path.

When she told me, "You forget how far you've come. Can we look at it together? Because I am so tremendously amazed by you."

ACCESSING HOPE

Accessing hope is not always easy, especially for folks in acute settings such as the foster care system, inpatient treatment, prison, or mental hospitals. These clients often have encompassing needs that extend far beyond what any therapeutic hour can provide.

If you work with clients in these settings, you probably

regularly ask yourself, *How can my work be relevant if a client doesn't have stable housing? What's the point of talking about emotions when someone's parent physically assaults them? When someone has endured a lifetime of trauma, how can one therapist even make a difference?*

Even clients in more stable situations often face hopelessness. What if their depression or anxiety or PTSD isn't getting better? What if things never improve with their partner or child? What if there just isn't a good solution for their chronic pain?

Other global circumstances make it challenging to find hope. Senseless tragedies happen all the time. People experience complete anguish. How do you access hope when you feel inundated by someone's agonizing circumstances?

First, we want to clarify that we differentiate between hope and toxic positivity. Toxic positivity refers to continually denying or rejecting negative experiences. It's a forced optimism that can mirror generic platitudes like *Everything happens for a reason* and *It'll all be okay.*

Good therapy does not sugarcoat pain or invalidate life adversity. Some client situations are that dire, and some pain is that unbearable.

Many clients need to feel the gravity of their hopelessness. At that point—and every point—it becomes your job to hold on to hope for them. Sometimes this looks like consciously choosing to avoid falling into indifference. You can't stop caring about your client's well-being, recovery, or healing. You have to find a beacon of light for your client. It doesn't matter how dim that light is or how far away it feels. But you have to find something and hold on to it fiercely.

If you don't, you stop believing therapy even matters for this client. At best, you might find yourself shifting into autopilot, drudging through your sessions. But at its worst, your apathy can lead you to judge, resent, or inadvertently stunt the treatment process altogether.

Our work always calls for hope. Therapy without hope is venting without resolution.

Here are some reminders for times when you find it hard to access hope:

Trust that the human species is resilient and capable: This has been proven in every generation. Bad things happen, but it would be remiss to overlook all of humanity's exquisiteness. If you find yourself losing hope or slipping into indifference, look for hints of resilience and strength. Consider all that your client has had to endure to get to where they are today. Consider how they have survived in the best ways they knew how. Allow yourself to reflect on all the unique virtues they exhibit.

Find glimmers: Deb Dana, who has written numerous books about polyvagal theory, introduced the concept of *glimmers* to describe micro-moments that promote a sense of hope, connection, and happiness. In a *Newsweek* article, she said, "Glimmers are all around waiting for us to bump into them, to find them, become aware of them, they're just these little moments that exist all over the place."[1] Holding on to hope sometimes means identifying glimmers with clients. This means learning more about what motivates or intrigues them. It also means paying attention to what makes them feel happy or connected to others. Glimmers can be so tiny, but everybody has them, and we can actualize hope when people trust that more glimmers are waiting in their future.

Lean on neuroplasticity: Dan Siegel, a well-known psychiatrist and author who's written extensively on the concept of neuroplasticity, emphasizes how the brain is malleable and continues growing throughout the lifespan. His neuroplasticity data contradicts former beliefs that the brain was essentially fixed after reaching a specific age. Research now shows that the brain can sculpt new neural pathways when people consistently change their responses. In other words, even the clients who seem most traumatized or unfixable can change.[2] Synthesizing both Viktor Frankl's and Siegel's contributions to this field, we'd add that hope as a therapist is about being willing to trust that change can happen. When it comes to your clients, any prevailing narrative can still be revised and rewritten.

Absorb what you love about your client: We are using the word *love* intentionally. Spend time internally reflecting on what you love about your client. If you can't think of anything right now, reflect until you can. Reframe this as part of your job. You have to find the good in the clients you work with. When you can integrate that good, hope often shows up. Once you have that insight, keep it close to you, and continue adding to it.

Remember that hope sometimes comes from validating hopelessness: You can't control your client's circumstances or their feelings. Life may be dark, and you can sit in the dark cave with them. By choosing to acknowledge deep pain, you help undo some of the aloneness. This, in many ways, can foster a sense of hope, as your client may internalize the notion that *even though it's terrible, someone is here for me. I don't have to do this all by myself.*

Step out of indifference: Indifference is one of the most unspoken detriments of therapy. You may not be able to change your client or the reality of their life, but you do have to care about them. If you struggle with indifference toward a client, make space to process your feelings with other providers or with your therapist. If it's a recurrent theme in your work, it may be a sign of burnout, which we cover extensively in part III.

Prioritize feel-good stories: Terrible things happen constantly, and we hear their magnitude in our work. We can all get bogged down by hopelessness, especially when working with clients who are experiencing immense hardship. But we must also notice and absorb what makes the world stunning. Prioritize seeking feel-good stories regularly, not just as a remedy to counteract devastating stories. Find your anchor that makes it possible to believe in the goodness of humanity. It's okay to swim away from that anchor, particularly during hard moments, but know where it rests at all times.

Honor the seeds you plant: In your work, you share insights and suggestions with your clients. Even if they don't change right away, their neural pathways absorb your words. Sometimes you get to see the first buds. Sometimes not. If you have to choose to believe in anything as a therapist, believe that hope matters.

How You Attune

Psychiatrist Karen Hopenwasser defines *attunement* as "a synchronized awareness of implicit knowing that is nonlinear and bidirectional. Empathically attuned clinicians are like microtonal tuning forks. They resonate with a variety of emotional pitches and will resonate with nuanced shifting of emotional tone."[3]

We love this exquisite definition. However, we also recognize that it's verbose and may seem more whimsical than applicable. In this section, we simplify what attunement means and how it can be translated into your work.

Have you ever felt like someone totally understands you? What do they do that makes you feel so understood? Chances are, they *attune*. They can read your verbal and nonverbal cues and respond to those cues accordingly. You experience moments of wondrous connection in ways that sometimes overshadow words.

Therapeutic attunement is dyadic and collaborative. You experience it *with* your client, meaning it is emotional and kinesthetic, experienced in the body and absorbed in the mind. All successful intimate relationships entail some degree of attunement. Although a client rarely uses this specific jargon to describe transformative treatment, they cite its merit often.

Going back to our online survey question about the most defining moments in therapy, here are some responses that speak to attunement:

My therapist notices when I dissociate and will ask, "Where did you go just now?" It makes me feel like they're really there and really seeing me.

She asked if she could sit next to me when I was talking about something hard. I had really wanted her to sit next to me but felt too nervous to ask. It's like she just sensed it.

He says, "It wasn't your fault," at exactly the times I desperately need to hear it most.

She cried with me. It made me feel like my story mattered and that my pain was warranted.

We highlighted earlier how children can develop secure attachments when their caregivers consistently and appropriately respond to their needs. This all hinges on attunement. A baby can't talk, but a stable caregiver seeks to attune to different types of cries and body movements to care for the child. Caregivers also attune to their baby's eating, sleeping, and playing routines, creating a predictable and safe rhythm in the home.

This involves a bidirectional process, where babies also become attuned to how their caregivers will respond. When positive consistency is displayed, the child is more likely to grow up trusting that their needs matter and can be met.

As therapists, we must strive to attune to our clients as much as possible. To be clear, in our efforts to co-regulate, we can't fully meet each need. That would be unrealistic. Our clients also are not infants who can't fend for themselves. However, we do seek to show our clients we are eagerly there for them. We achieve this in many ways, including via direct actions, chosen words, body language, and the specific ways we choose to intervene.

Many clients come to therapy feeling completely alone in their experiences. They talk about feeling ashamed, vulnerable, misunderstood, rejected, and afraid. How many times have you heard the phrases "I feel crazy" or "This is fucked up, but...""?

Attunement is what offers clients the power to be seen. Furthermore, it is what shows them they are not crazy and that their feelings, needs, and experiences are not wrong. This is the very basis of what makes therapy so transformative.

ATTUNING TO TRANSFERENCE

Therapists can provide impressionable, relational experiences for their clients. This corresponds with the term *corrective emotional experience*, first coined in 1946 by psychoanalysts Franz Alexander and Thomas Morton French.[4]

The idea is that in treatment, you respond differently to a client's pain or story than others have in the past. You might strive to be compassionate and validating, often to the client's surprise. You don't wince when they share something that feels embarrassing to them. You hold the consistency even when they panic or pull away.

Although clients often logically know a therapist *should* be supportive, that doesn't mean their nervous system isn't anticipating your rejection or abandonment. If your client has been hurt in the past, it only makes sense for them to expect history to repeat itself. People want to keep themselves safe. They don't want to risk getting hurt again, and why, from their perspective, should you be any different from those who harmed them?

Repeated corrective emotional experiences in therapy can help people change their perceptions about themselves and others. This can support healing from past hardships. If your clients can internalize corrective emotional experiences, they may then be able to respond to triggers differently in their daily lives. They can take what you offer and integrate it into other relationships.

Psychoanalyst Heinz Kohut believed that therapists needed to offer their clients corrective emotional experiences through empathy and attunement. He delineated how engaging in different transferences could support this process.[5] Although we recognize that not all therapists focus on transference in therapy, being aware of these dynamics may help you better practice attunement in your daily work.

Here are a few different types of transference to consider:

Mirroring transference: This type derives from the concept that all children need to feel special and wanted by their caregivers. They yearn for unconditional love; threats to that love can feel devastating. Therapists can support helping clients fulfill this need by regularly reflecting, acknowledging, praising, applauding, and valuing their efforts. While you can't make anyone feel a certain way, many clients want to feel like they matter and that they are important to you.

Idealizing transference: This type relates to the concept of children admiring their caregivers and perceiving them to be safe, powerful, and competent. While not all clients will idealize their therapists, some will certainly put you on a pedestal. Over time, however, it can be beneficial for clients to develop a more accurate perception of your limits and flaws. This is where the heart of your humanness thrives. Clients need to know that you're not perfect, and they also need to trust that your imperfection isn't a bad thing.

Twinship transference: This type speaks to how children realize they share valuable characteristics with their caregivers. This connectivity creates a sense of belonging and collaboration. The child also looks for other affirming relationships outside of the home. In therapy, this looks like you and your client feeling more like equals and your client wanting to emulate what feels *good* in therapy by bringing it into the outside world.

At this point, despite the many parent-child parallels we

have shared, we emphatically note that therapists are not substitute parents. This is a very good thing. Even the most compassionate parent can't remain fully attuned to their child's well-being in every interaction. A parent's life is filled with too many other competing demands, including other children, sinks full of dishes, emails that need to be answered, and school paperwork that must be filled out.

Therapy offers a unique experience. The time constraints and boundaries do allow you to give your clients undivided attention. Every single time.

This is a key difference between a therapeutic relationship and other relationships. You are hired and paid to hyperfocus on your client's well-being every moment they spend with you. For that hour, you can be completely, wholeheartedly invested in knowing them and being with their stories and feelings. Because it is not reciprocal, they get the experience of being wholly cared for—without having to offer anything in return.

Attunement in Action

Attunement starts with paying close attention and listening fully. In graduate school, you learned about the importance of listening, but people often forget its relevance. No theory or elaborate training replicates *showing up and listening*. However, many of your clients will come to you feeling like nobody has really listened to them. Instead, they often feel misunderstood or unsupported. Without listening, you can't attune.

In *Beyond Empathy*, authors Richard Erskine, Janet Moursund, and Rebecca Trautmann outline how attunement comes in four layers:[6]

> **Affective attunement:** Affective attunement means focusing on your client's affect. You note their nonverbal

communication and pay close attention to shifts in their facial expressions, gestures, eye contact, tone of voice, facial flushing or dislocation, or posturing. These shifts could indicate the presence of important emotions like anger, fear, or shame that could otherwise be missed if you're solely focusing on words. To address these shifts, you might say, "I see the moistness in your eyes" or "Your voice got a little louder there. This sounds like it's important." These statements indicate your ability to track the moment-to-moment shifts occurring in session. They can affirm the significance of what is happening directly in the here and now, which can help clients slow down and become more aware of their inner experiences.

Cognitive attunement: Cognitive attunement is about seeking to understand your client's meanings and perspectives. This often comes in the form of reflections, such as "It sounds like you . . ." or "What I'm hearing is that you . . ." or "I can imagine this made you feel . . ." At this point, you are attempting to validate certain experiences while also offering insights. Your clients have the right to agree or disagree with these statements. Either way, this bid for attunement creates space for deeper processing.

When you engage in cognitive attunement, you're drawing a connection between the stated content and how you experience it. When executed well, it demonstrates deep listening and helps clients expand their awareness.

Developmental attunement: Developmental attunement means deliberately engaging with your client's presenting developmental state. This can be especially important when your client is in a regressed state and feeling or acting younger than they are. This doesn't mean treating an adult like a child. Instead, it means you strive to hold compassion for that part of them instead of judging or asking them to shift away from that state.

Developmental attunement is a more advanced type of attunement and can be harder to implement. Regardless of which theoretical orientation you embrace, it is a good idea to try to understand which developmental needs your client may not have had met. This is especially important when working with clients with developmental or attachment-based traumas.

Rhythmic attunement: Rhythmic attunement refers to mirroring your client's natural rhythms. For example, if your client is crying and speaking slowly about a challenging topic, you might slow your own pace and speak in a quieter tone. When your client becomes animated when talking about something exciting to them, you might match your energy to share their excitement with them. This type of matching is a form of mirroring, and it's an important part of maintaining an intimate connection.

HOW WELL DO YOU NEED TO ATTUNE?

Attunement is part of the mentalization process of therapy. Psychologist and professor Peter Fonagy describes mentalization as the desire to seek, understand, and imagine another person's thoughts. It's the conscious act of having someone's mind in mind.[7]

A young child depends on their caregiver to care about, attend to, and *attune* to their mental states. This helps them distinguish their inner reality from the world around them, and it supports the development of a secure attachment to self and others.

But let's talk about what happens when you get it wrong—because you might be reading this section and thinking it all sounds good (or overly complex) in theory. What if you misinterpret your client's needs? What if you acknowledge seeing the moistness in their eyes, and they say they just have allergies? What if you tell someone you're proud of them, and they get upset because their mother only praised them when they accomplished something, and now you've reminded them of this past trigger? Or what if you mention how moved you feel by your client's story, but they interpret it as you finding their story to be too intense for you to handle?

These tense moments occur often and quickly in therapy. As we emphasized earlier, perfection isn't possible. It isn't even a virtuous goal. All therapists get it wrong because all people get it wrong. Ruptures can and do occur within therapy, and that's why CHAIR also emphasizes the need for repair, which we dive into in chapter 7.

We have talked about how secure attachment develops for babies. But it's a misconception that even the best parents are attuned at all times. As mentioned, parents have so many competing responsibilities. Even when they love their child dearly, sometimes they have no choice but to let them cry a few moments too long. At other times, they make a judgment call on behalf of their child only to realize, in hindsight, that they could have made a better choice.

Psychologist Edward Tronick, who is best known for his famous "Still Face Experiment," shows what happens when mothers are unresponsive to their babies. His videos show how children become distressed or helpless when their mothers continuously show a blank expression. Fortunately, the child tends to recover quickly once the mother resumes a receptive range of facial expressions.

Tronick's research on mother-child dyads reveals another

interesting observation. He found that only about 20%–30% of all interactions are completely matched synchronously.[8] In other words, it can be theorized that the majority of effective connection isn't just about being in sync—it's about how people move back into sync after they step out of it.

British pediatrician and psychoanalyst Donald Winnicott embraced the notion of imperfection within families. He suggested that "good enough" parenting simultaneously honors a mother's dedication to her child while acknowledging her inherent unreliability as a human being.

Therapy isn't about constant attunement. It's about the curiosity and intention to attune. It's also about what you deliberately do with clients if misattunement occurs.

In the context of therapy, even with the best intentions in mind, you can't wholly attune to every client's emotional state or need. But when you are generally receptive and tracking your client's responses, such disparities can be resolved. At other times, and in more complex cases, ruptures can occur, which we will discuss shortly.

We can conceptualize that the process of *getting back into attunement* is more important than *always staying attuned*. After all, nobody is a mind reader, and this applies to even the very best therapist. Your willingness to identify and even rectify moments of misattunement creates a foundation for building secure relationships with your clients.

Your overarching goal of attunement should be to convey that you see, hear, and care about your client. This includes using explicit language, but it also lives in how you carry yourself in sessions. When you do this well, clients feel witnessed and understood. They can sit back and think, *My therapist just gets me.* You want your clients to feel like you get them, and if you don't have this sense, you want to figure out what might be causing a blockage.

Attunement guides interventions and guides the role you play within the relationship. This leads to effective therapeutic impact, which we discuss in the next chapter.

Specific Guidelines for Strengthening Attunement Skills

- Practice paying very close attention to nonverbal communication. Even if you don't explicitly address it, get in the habit of tracking shifts in tone, eye contact, body posturing, and facial expressions. Make note that these shifts may indicate important entry points for attunement.

- No matter which theoretical orientation you resonate with, remember that every type of therapy has a relational element to it. There is a reason therapists generally learn the basic skills of active listening, empathy, validation, and building rapport *first*. These allow you to facilitate the attunement process, and they are the most essential skills you can have. They can never be understated, and they can always be strengthened.

- Prioritize how it might feel to be in your client's shoes. If you can't understand what life in their shoes might feel like, you may need to ask more clarifying questions to better understand their story or needs. The more you have context for why someone does what they do, the more empathy and compassion you can have for their struggles or behaviors.

- Always think about what a client needs most from you. If you're not sure, consider the merit of asking them directly with questions like "How can I support you right now?" or "What can I offer you in this moment?" or "How can we make the most of this time together today?"

- If you can't meet your client's identified need, collaborate on how you can still support them *and* empower them so they can strive to meet that need outside of therapy. Sometimes it's enough to say, "I'm so sorry that I can't change this, but I am right here."

- Remember that attunement is an imperfect process, and the goal is never to be an expert on the client's life. Instead, it is a trial-and-error process of actively trying to *get* attuned instead of assuming attunement is a default state. It can be good practice to check in on the validity of your observations with clients by asking, "Correct me if I'm wrong" or "To me, it sounds like . . . , but how does that sound to you?"

- Practice attunement in everyday life. This is a skill that every human benefits from. Deepening your ability to attune to loved ones can improve your relationships and overall sense of well-being, and you will carry that with you through your work. With that, be mindful of the risk of only giving without receiving. It's equally important to prioritize spending time with people who attune well to you.

CHAPTER 6

WHAT MAKES
THERAPY IMPACTFUL?

We seek impact. We all want someone or something to change our life for the better. So many of us are searching for *something* to affect us so profoundly that it motivates us to make *that* change we need to make. This is why many of us are drawn to self-help books, rejuvenating retreats, and prominent podcasts. It's also why celebrities and social media influencers hold such immense authority in daily life. We want solutions for our problems, and we're drawn to self-improvement and self-healing. Even if they don't know exactly what change looks like, many clients do enter therapy expecting you to have an impact on them.

Let's go back to the responses we generated from our discussion question, *What was the most defining moment of your therapy treatment?*

Any and all parts of the CHAIR framework affect clients. Your consistency can spur change. Your willingness to attune to their needs or hold hope when life feels impossible can also make a profound difference. Combining such skills supercharges your capacity to impact clients.

In this chapter, we focus exclusively on our concept of deliberate therapeutic impact. We define *therapeutic impact* as the specific ways you seek to shift your client's way of thinking, experiencing, or relating within treatment.

Because *therapeutic impact* is such a broad term, we decided to break up the 19,000 responses into four subcategories with the following prevailing themes: unfolding of trust, therapist self-disclosure, connecting the pieces, and moments between.

Unfolding of trust: Honoring the cadence and pace of how your clients learn to trust you

Therapist self-disclosure: Discerning whether, when, and what to share about your personal life with your clients

Connecting the pieces: Identifying and processing insights about the client that they may not have readily seen or understood before therapy

Moments between: Relishing the playful and light human interactions with your client

All of our choices as therapists carry inherent risk in terms of their potential impact. Some clients may vehemently disagree with the information we present. Others might agree with the insight being offered, but accepting the truth evokes pain or shame, causing them to withdraw from us or the treatment altogether.

As we have emphasized throughout, making mistakes is inevitable in every clinical practice. Sometimes the flow of therapy feels disjointed. The quality of the therapeutic relationship matters at every point and in every interaction—rapport and safety are paramount. When clients feel secure with you, ideally they can trust that what you offer is intended to help.

Avoiding having an impact on our clients can be risky too. This plays out when clients make remarks like *All that therapist did was smile and nod* or *They were nice, but they didn't really help.*

Clients do want support and kindness, but they also value thinking about themselves and the world differently. After all, they're in therapy because something needs to change.

UNFOLDING OF TRUST

The most defining moment was when I told him something I'd never told anyone. I had finally gotten to a space where I trusted that he could handle it, and he absolutely did handle it.

The most defining moment was when I realized I trusted her. It took three years for me to reach that point. Once I was there, I felt like I had landed in this incredible safety.

The most defining moment was when she said I didn't have to talk if I didn't want to talk. I trusted that she respected my process.

Therapists often take trust for granted, talking breezily about the benefits of valuing a trusting relationship with clients. They assure clients they can be trusted with their secrets or fears. They emphasize that healing is difficult if trust isn't in place.

But trust isn't an all-or-nothing experience, and it isn't a destination that's just *achieved* in therapy. It's a fluid experience that sometimes vacillates throughout the work.

Sometimes clients will lie or distort the truth about themselves. In fact, research shows that 93% of clients admit to lying in therapy.[1] Clients lie to skilled therapists, and they lie despite really wanting to be honest and improve the quality of their lives. Many lie and still have an excellent relationship with their therapist. Lying doesn't inherently mean your client doesn't trust you. Instead, it means your client likely has deeper, long-standing fears that are much greater than their relationship with you.

If you think you can accurately assess when a client is lying to you, you're probably wrong. Research also shows that our ability to discern lies is no more accurate than flipping a coin; this finding is seen across numerous populations, from students to judges to job interviewers to therapists. Even lie detection technology remains questionable. The American Psychological Association stated that polygraph tests are controversial and may not hold much validity at all.[2]

Clients might lie for many reasons. They want you to like them or be impressed with their progress. They prefer to believe embellished narratives instead of the raw truth. They fear that what really happened is too much for someone else to handle. They worry about your rejecting or abandoning them.

Many people may move through life lying to themselves, and those lies grow legs that walk into therapy sessions. Sometimes clients withhold the truth because they don't even realize that a certain truth is relevant to treatment. Therefore, they feel no need to share it with you.

We perceive that deceit is always an act of survival and self-preservation. People lie when the cost of the truth feels steeper than the cost of the lie. Assuming that your clients probably lie to you in some form, how do you still try to promote a safe environment? What does trust mean in this context, and is it necessary for promoting honesty or even achieving treatment success?

EARNING TRUST

No form of trust comes automatically. Clients with trauma histories often face even more complex challenges when it comes to trust. Why bother opening up, they might think, if you could hurt them? What if they tell you something that makes them vulnerable and you reject or criticize their feelings? Furthermore, medical mistrust is real and valid. Many clients fear that if they tell you the truth about what's occurring in their lives, it could result in serious consequences, including involuntary hospitalization or having their children taken from them. Clients know that therapists have legal and ethical obligations to report abuse, neglect, and the imminent risk of harm to themselves or others. Some clients worry about how that kind of professional power could be used against them.

You could be a world-class therapist, but even that doesn't guarantee trust. What if your client was recently betrayed and still feels unsteady around others? What if they worked with another therapist who made a negligent mistake? What if, like so many clients, they have a massive fear of abandonment?

It always makes sense for clients to feel cautious about therapy. They also have a right to be choosy about their provider and selective about the type of therapy itself. This is especially true at the onset of treatment. Your ability to maintain positive consistency and attunement sets a foundation for trust to unfold. It is your job to convey a genuine experience where the connection doesn't feel like some dicey gamble.

But you aren't a detective. Therapy isn't about discerning

truth from lies or facts from fiction. Sometimes your client won't even know which is which. Instead, therapy sometimes means building a relationship in which you can welcome any fear, skepticism, and uncertainty toward you or the treatment.

In all that you do with your clients, it is important to wholeheartedly respect the scaffolding of trust. Trust is malleable, often developing over time, and successful therapy can still thrive even when a client trusts you only partially. Assuming that a client must fully trust you (or therapy itself) often leads to unrealistic expectations. If you provide short-term or crisis management work, you won't have time to earn complete trust. You have to work quickly, even if the rapport isn't as deep or strong as you'd like.

Think about how many people you wholeheartedly trust. Probably not too many. Now think about how many people know your greatest secrets and darkest shame. Your number has gotten even lower. It may even be zero. There are reasons for this, and all those reasons are legitimate.

Trust is extraordinarily hard, so we must all honor every defense and fear clients bring to therapy. Here are some ways to respect the unfolding and earning of trust:

Guidelines for Respecting the Unfolding of Trust

- Be mindful about hyper-focusing on whether clients are being fully honest with you. Instead, understand that most people omit, embellish, or lie when they feel threatened. Don't take it personally if and when clients engage in this way with you. Use CHAIR to offer your consistent, hopeful, and attuned presence. Clients may feel more inclined to tell the truth when it simply feels safe for them to do so.

- Consider eliminating the word *resistance* from your therapist vocabulary. When you feel tempted to use this word for a client who may present as guarded, dismissive, or rejecting, think about how you might honor the part of them that questions compliance or challenges you. Resistance is often just a label for fear or shame.

- Look for cues that your client might be trusting you more (sharing more vulnerable content, revealing a greater variety of emotional expressions, acknowledging their own obstacles or fears around trust). These cues may feel slight, but they are always worth noting. If a client is opening up, keep leaning into attunement. You want to show that you are paying close attention to their content *and* their affect and that you honor their willingness to trust you.

- Consider highlighting the relational component of trust in therapy with questions like "What's it like for you to share this with me?" or "How do you feel talking about this with me right now?" These questions can also highlight where mistrust or shame may be present.

- Validate fears about trust. Understand where they come from. Never force a client to talk about something if they don't feel ready to talk about it.

- Go to your own therapy and practice being 100% honest at all times. We bet you can't do it! But think about what makes it hard for you to trust your own therapist. If you aren't in therapy yourself, notice when it's challenging for you to trust others (even when you logically know they are safe to confide in).

- When in doubt, focus on the first tenets of CHAIR: consistency, hope, and attunement. This is what you can control. Your client controls whether they choose to trust you. They have that right at all times. You don't get to make that choice for anyone.

- Always be willing to acknowledge your mistakes and repair any ruptures if they occur. Chapter 7 offers more guidelines on this topic.

SELF-DISCLOSURE

Many respondents to our survey said their therapist's self-disclosure was a pivotal point in treatment. This finding did not surprise us, as self-disclosure can build rapport, and it can also demonstrate your sense of humility and relatability as a therapist.

No matter where you stand on self-disclosure, it is impossible to reveal nothing about yourself. Clients draw assumptions based on whatever details they can gather, including the clothes you wear and specific words you choose. They notice wedding rings and tattoos and how long you take a vacation, and they pay attention to the photos on your website or marketing materials. They constantly assess who you are as both a therapist and a real person. This is what psychologist Ofer Zur and colleagues have cited as *unavoidable self-disclosure*. You can't help but share it.[3]

Some clients will want to know more about your life,

prompting them to ask you direct questions. For example, a teenager might ask you about your specific taste in music, or a grieving client may ask you if you've ever experienced a traumatic death. Couples often ask if you're married, just as parents often ask if you have children. Specific branches of curiosity differ from client to client, but questions about your personal life often come from a place that sounds like *Can you understand this important part of me?*

Modern society has dramatically shifted clinicians away from blank-slate therapy. Today, most of us have some form of online visibility. This may be where you consciously choose to integrate your lived experiences or personal biases as part of your professional identity. From this perspective, your humanness represents a part of your therapeutic branding. Before a first session, a client might know that you have autism or OCD or that you like backpacking or doing improv in your free time. Sometimes clients will reach out to you because your self-disclosure led them to believe you could help them.

Research shows that more than 90% of therapists disclose personal information to clients.[4] While therapists often contemplate how, when, or what to share, the nature of self-disclosure has long remained a contentious topic in the psychotherapy field.

Impactful self-disclosure can:

- Help clients feel more connected to you
- Offer a deep sense of validation
- Cultivate trust
- Provide a sense of hope
- Maintain the fabric of a meaningful therapeutic relationship

Your expertise makes you a therapist. Clients want to trust

your competence. But many will also be curious about your humanness. This makes sense—it's natural to be interested in the person you're sharing every sharp fear or insecurity with. This inquisitiveness can also come from a vulnerable place that says, *Who are you, really? Do you have any idea what this pain feels like?* and *Whether you do or don't, can you actually be there to help me?* Sometimes clients also grapple with a script that reads, *I'm scared and feel like you're too good or too perfect, and I need to know that you sometimes struggle too.*

This curiosity can also come from a lighter place. As humans, we all like to find what makes us similar to others. It provides a sense of validation and belonging. A client might feel more connected knowing that you share a similar taste in movies or that you traveled to the place where they're going on vacation next week. We will share some of the responses we received that illuminate the benefits of self-disclosure.

One interviewee told us, *I had already quit drinking when I started working with my therapist. But my recovery felt very shaky, and it made me feel embarrassed and insecure. When she told me she was in recovery from an addiction herself, it opened my capacity to trust her. I would have never known, as she came across as so calm and composed. It was one of the most important parts of our work together.*

Another shared about being in therapy for the indescribable grief she felt after giving birth to her stillborn daughter. This client specifically chose a provider who had openly noted her own experience of losing a child. The client told us, *It was the worst pain I ever endured. I truly don't think anyone can understand what it is like unless they've been through it. Knowing she also went through it never made the pain better, but it did make me feel less alone. I had permission to fully feel my emotions without filtering my words. I absolutely had to have this kind of space.*

One more said simply, *The most defining moment was when my therapist told me she also had ADHD. I felt so seen.*

Another said, *I'm a therapist myself, and I asked my therapist if she had ever experienced suicidal thoughts. I expected her to deflect the question or explore why her answer was important to me. Instead, she just held my gaze and said, "Oh, yes."*

RISKS OF SELF-DISCLOSURE

The appropriate use of self-disclosure helps validate a client's experience and ideally evokes further introspection. It is an intervention that showcases your humanness in an effort to strengthen rapport. In many ways, it says, *I'm not a robot. I'm a human too. We're both human in this experience.* But despite your humanness, it is paramount to avoid making therapy about yourself. Inappropriate self-disclosure can happen when you seek to satisfy your needs more than your client's needs.

You can lean on your personal history or desires as a basic reference point. But your *personal stuff* can't be a central compass point of treatment. Carelessly sharing about your life can cause clients to feel responsible for your well-being. It can also make therapy feel too casual and friend-like. This dynamic can cause clients to call your expertise into question. Clients will experience inappropriate self-disclosure as annoying, uncomfortable, or awkward. Self-disclosure can be inappropriate when it's:

Overly lengthy and specific in detail: If you choose to share something about yourself, it's generally a best practice to keep it brief and general.

Unclear how it might benefit the client's well-being: If you can't fully identify why it's helpful for your client to have this information, it may not be appropriate to share.

Irrelevant to the topic at hand: When you feel the impulse to share something that is disconnected from the current conversation, this may be more about satisfying your need rather than your client's.

Coming from a place of assuming you know what a client needs or how a client feels based on your own experience: Be mindful of overidentifying with clients. You may personally resonate with parts of their story and want to connect with them based on your experience. However, it's often more meaningful to attempt to fully understand their perspective rather than home in on how you relate to it.

The only way you feel you can relate to your clients: Self-disclosure can be a wonderful tool. But if it's your primary tool, you risk causing clients to feel that therapy is more about your talking about yourself than genuinely helping them with their presenting concerns.

In addition, self-disclosure is one of those facets of therapy that is highly nuanced and client-specific. One client may value knowing a great deal about your life. Someone else won't want to know a single detail. You will also have clients who only want answers to questions they directly ask. You won't always get self-disclosure right, but you should be mindful of all the risks and benefits before you do it.

Reflection Questions before Self-Disclosing Information to a Client

- What is my intended purpose for self-disclosing at this time in treatment?
- Why am I choosing to self-disclose instead of engaging in another intervention?
- How would I defend my decision to self-disclose this information to a supervisor or other therapist inquiring why I made this choice?
- How do I feel knowing that once I share this information with my client, it can never be undone, and I can't control whether my client shares it with others?
- What risks can I identify that are associated with this self-disclosure?
- How will I assess how effective this self-disclosure was for my client's overall treatment?

CONNECTING THE PIECES

The work of therapy often resembles solving a thousand-piece jigsaw puzzle without the picture for reference. You are given some assorted pieces at intake, and you receive a few more each session, but you only have about one hour each week to work with your client to connect the pieces together.

To amplify the pressure, you may need to work on this puzzle while also being scrutinized by many outsiders, including your client's family members, teachers, spouses, insurance company utilization reviewers, probation officers, and more. Everyone, it seems, will want you to finish the puzzle as quickly as possible.

But humans, unlike jigsaw puzzles, are remarkably elaborate, and the limited time you spend with a client will never last long enough to fit all one thousand pieces together. You can't access all one thousand pieces in the course of treatment. Despite how open and honest a client is, nobody can truly share every piece of their life puzzle with another person.

Therefore, one of your goals with clients is to collaborate effectively with them. What puzzle picture do they wish to create? Which pieces do they really want to work on? What pieces already fit well together, and which pieces might need to be discarded altogether?

The puzzle metaphor goes even deeper.

Which pieces did they once have that no longer fit in their life? How have they tried to solve their puzzle in the past? Which pieces look like they should fit together but, upon closer inspection, just don't make a good match? Who has criticized their puzzle or their attempts to work on their puzzle? How comfortable do they feel working on this puzzle with *you*?

For example, let's say a young woman, Maria, comes to you because she feels depressed. She is overwhelmed at work and frustrated that she and her husband continue fighting. She claims he isn't sensitive to her mental health needs, although he did support her seeking treatment. Maria tells you that her goal is to "feel better about life." These are the presented puzzle pieces, although they may only equate to about a dozen pieces out of a thousand.

You don't really know Maria yet. You only know those dozen pieces. So, where do you start? You might focus exclusively on Maria's history of depression and how it has affected her well-being. You might pay closer attention to the state of her marriage and her current role as a wife. You could feel inclined to learn more about Maria's family and her parents' role in shaping and supporting her mental health.

Each of these entry points is valid. As we mentioned in chapter 2, therapists must regularly grapple with the perils of decision fatigue and decision paralysis. The abundance of options can be daunting, and there's certainly no superior way to intervene with Maria. But this is where we want to highlight what it means to address blind spots, and how it's one of the best gifts we can offer our clients.

CONNECTING THERAPEUTIC PUZZLE PIECES

To highlight this unique concept, we introduce the well-known Johari Window, a communications framework developed by Joseph Luft and Harry Ingham in 1955.[5] As you can see in the illustration below, this window consists of four quadrants, including the open area, blind spot, hidden area, and unknown.

Johari Window Model

	Known to self	Not known to self
Known to others	Open area	Blind spot
Not known to others	Hidden area	Unknown

Open area: The open area is the most conscious part of the self. It contains all that a client knows about themselves and is willing to disclose to others. In the above situation, Maria's open area includes her depression, work stress, and marital issues. She is open about those symptoms and experiences, and others may also be able to detect them easily.

Blind spot: The blind spot is just what it sounds like. It consists of the traits and patterns that others see that are unknown to the client. For example, if you and Maria were to continue working together, you might note that she tends to default to logic and reasoning instead of permitting herself to experience emotion. You might observe a pattern of her justifying her husband's criticism while holding back tears. You may even see how she cancels therapy during the weeks after she has particularly difficult sessions. If Maria is unaware of these tendencies, this information stays within the blind spot quadrant.

Hidden area: The hidden area refers to the information clients keep concealed from others. Earlier, we spoke about themes of mistrust and dishonesty in therapy. This area falls into that category. But any experience or emotion can arise here. Shame is most likely to be in this space. For example, Maria might omit that she sometimes contemplates ending her life when her depression symptoms feel unbearable. She might also avoid sharing how she sometimes lashes out at others when she reaches a particular emotional threshold. This information is tucked away in the dark and seemingly removed from the rest of her puzzle.

Unknown: The unknown quadrant refers to all the behaviors, patterns, or motives undetectable to both you and your client. For example, maybe neither Maria nor you know that Maria's deceased mother also had depression that closely resembles some of her symptoms. Perhaps you both don't know that her husband is having an affair, and his slight withdrawal from the marriage is one of the catalysts driving Maria's depression. This data belongs in the unknown area, as neither of you is aware of its existence.

It can't be your job to try to read a client's mind or assume a detective's stance in session. With that, you also can't be naive in believing you have access to a completed thousand-piece puzzle when working with clients. No matter how strong your rapport is, there will always be surprises and uncertainties.

So, let's talk about how treatment can progress from here. Therapy typically begins by joining with your clients in their open area. You establish an initial alliance and talk about safe topics that clients feel comfortable sharing. This lays the initial foundation for a good working relationship.

But you can't stay in this quadrant indefinitely. Your client is already familiar with the landscape in their open area. They live there. It's as familiar to them as their name and birthday. They're coming to therapy because they need help with the rest of their puzzle.

Throughout treatment, you must continually consider all the quadrants. This is where all professional ingredients, including your expertise, conceptualization skills, peer consultation, supervision, and personal intuition, come together. You are hired to help clients understand their blind spots. When you do this effectively and compassionately, you can offer the gift of tremendous impact.

Discerning and Identifying Blind Spots

)y identifying any observations or
nation you *sense* could be beneficial to the
client that they may not know about. Keep in mind
that every theoretical orientation has some
language identifying how clients get stuck (e.g.,
cognitive distortions, defense mechanisms,
enmeshment, target memories).

- Pay attention to discrepancies in your client's
  verbal and nonverbal behavior. Note times when
  their emotions seem particularly heightened or
  even out of character. Try to track behavioral
  patterns in how they relate to you. Consider how
  these themes may play out in other relationships in
  the client's life.

- Note any insights that you may wrongfully assume
  your client knows. For example, you might *assume* a
  client knows what a healthy boundary is or what
  anxiety symptoms look like. Just because
  something feels obvious to you does not mean it is
  obvious to your client. Psychoeducation can lead to
  raising awareness of blind spots.

- One of the simplest (and kindest) ways to offer
  insight into a blind spot is to introduce any tidbits
  by starting with "I wonder if . . ." or "I want to share
  something I've noticed." This gives the client the
  chance to ponder your reflection and offer you
  feedback about whether it sounds accurate or not.

- Keep in mind that clients may have some awareness of what exists in their blind spot. For example, your client might recognize that they have difficulty identifying feelings. Saying, "I can see how hard it is for you to just be with sadness" may gently tug at their intellectualizing blind spot. Deepening this insight can help you both connect other quadrants.

- Remember that 100% accuracy isn't necessarily the goal when sharing reflections or offering insights. Sometimes by getting it wrong, you open space for the client to correct you with the right information (which may be in their hidden facade).

- Remember that your goal is to help clients work on their puzzles. Present the pieces you have available and work together to connect pieces. This process is collaborative and dyadic. Together, through building these connections, you create meaning that can inspire clients to integrate new insights and make important changes in their lives.

Quadrants continually interconnect throughout therapy. For example, maybe Maria has lunch with her father. She opens up to him about going to therapy and acknowledges she's been struggling with depression. This prompts her father to mention that his late wife, Maria's mother, experienced similar mental health issues. Maria brings this revelation back into therapy with you. Now you have both acquired some new puzzle pieces that were previously in the unknown arena.

All good therapy requires some form of intervention that

moves, shakes, and connects pivotal puzzle pieces. These interventions facilitate movement among the various quadrants. For example, if you present a blind spot, this may touch significant information within the hidden area. That can pivot you both into the unknown, and discovering what lies there opens space for deeper exploration. The movement is in how pieces come together. It isn't always in the form of bold confrontations. Sometimes the process of connecting feels tender and soft. Sometimes it even happens accidentally. But in all cases, connecting a client's puzzle pieces comes from a place where you maintain respectful curiosity.

How did connecting the pieces show up in the replies to our question, *What was the most defining moment of your therapy treatment?* Here are a few responses that spoke to this theme:

She said, "You don't give yourself enough credit for your resilience." When we followed up in the survey and asked why that specifically felt so impactful, this person said, *Well, I had never seen myself as tough before. And then I was able to reflect on the ways I really have been resilient. And that opened some kind of confidence for me. It's like I could really believe in myself.*

In this example, the therapist offered insight in the blind spot quadrant. This led the client to enter the unknown arena. They were able to identify their resilience. This allowed them to connect more pieces, which impacted how they perceived themselves. This can lead to many positive outcomes, including changed behaviors and enhanced self-esteem.

Another person replied, *He asked, "Have you ever considered that what your friend is doing is a form of emotional abuse?" And, yeah, of course, I sorta did, deep down at least, but him bringing it right here in the room made me realize I couldn't hide from this very obvious truth anymore.*

This entailed the therapist addressing a blind spot,

although the blind spot may have been blurry rather than invisible. In confronting his denial, the client was then able to acknowledge that he couldn't ignore this painful reality anymore.

In another concise response, a respondent said, *My therapist said that it sounded like I don't really love my partner. This fucked me up for days, and it fucked me up because I'd always known it was true, and I just didn't want to admit it aloud.*

This clearly represents how a therapist identifying a blind spot can lead to a client acknowledging information within the hidden area. They had privately known something that they hadn't shared with anyone. From that vantage point, with new pieces on the table, both client and therapist can decide how they want to proceed together.

MOMENTS BETWEEN

The last cluster of responses to our question, *What was the most defining moment of your therapy treatment?* admittedly surprised us.

Among the 19,000 responses, we received thousands of seemingly random stories about nonclinical moments that had an immense impact on people. At first, we dismissed these replies. They didn't seem to hold as much weight as the first three types of responses: unfolding of trust, self-disclosure, and connecting the pieces.

One client shared that her defining moment was talking about a concert. She followed up and insisted on telling us that the conversation was not inherently therapeutic. She let us know that nothing about this interaction connected to her treatment goals, but she did say, *At this point, we had talked about everything dark. My bad childhood, my sexual abuse, my ongoing depression struggles. And she helped me in so many ways. But I also realized that, even though she knew all my pain, she knew very little about my happiness. As I talked to her about this concert, it was like I was able to connect how far I'd come. A couple of years ago, I wouldn't have been able to have such a good time.*

Other answers:

Seeing my therapist's cat on the telehealth screen.

When we both cracked up over our shared love for this obscure board game.

Showing her my baby pictures.

Playing with Play-Doh together.

You can see how these types of answers may seem random and disconnected from one another. But in conceptualizing their relevance, we landed on our working concept of the impact associated with the *moments between*.

The moments between are the moments of lightness, humor, play, offhand comments, brief small talk, and humanness that occur in the course of therapy. The moments between can serve to level out the power differential; more than anything, in these experiences, you are stepping into being a human with your human client.

ACKNOWLEDGING THE PLAYFULNESS AND LIGHTNESS

We once heard that a course of therapy can resemble a television series. The metaphor makes some sense. Sessions may look like episodes building upon one another, referencing previous episodes, interconnecting plots and subplots, and threading together common themes. Some episodes feel heavier or more dramatic than others. And some shows end in a single season, whereas others air for decades.

Your clients, of course, are not characters in a show. There is no script for them to follow and no arbitrary role for them to play. Anything is up for grabs. Some clients give you an abridged life story during the intake, and others wait years before divulging critical information. Neither approach is better or worse, but all therapists should be mindful that the often-idealized notion of "going as deep as possible" is not the same as being as effective as possible.

This is where therapists who work with younger children tend to thrive. They naturally honor the human desire for play, humor, and creative expression. They will sit on the floor and color pictures and play card games together. They recognize that not all conversations can be heavy or emotionally charged, and they trust children to lead the session accordingly, which speaks to the attunement process we referenced earlier.

Child therapists accept lightness as an inherent part of the work. Painting or listening to music isn't a waste of time. It's a matter of connecting and building and maintaining rapport. Most providers honor that children can't always express their feelings or talk about their thoughts candidly. However, they will show obvious signs of dysregulation. They might cry, throw a toy, or refuse to talk when their emotions are heightened. Therapists are mindful of this and can quickly pivot to helping their younger clients modulate their emotions when needed.

However, there's often much less tolerance for playfulness and lightness with adult clients. Therapists sometimes find themselves becoming impatient when a client won't talk about something serious. They also might worry that talking about a surface-level topic means that they are both avoiding the necessary work of therapy.

It's so tempting to focus solely on therapeutic breakthroughs as indicators of an impactful treatment. We define therapeutic breakthroughs as monumental moments that shift the course of therapy treatment. Your efforts to impact clients can facilitate breakthroughs, but breakthroughs are not the only evidence of therapeutic success.

In fact, too many of them clustered too close together can dysregulate a client. We explain this below.

LETTING GO OF CHASING AND COLLECTING BREAKTHROUGHS

Clients often want to achieve breakthroughs as much as therapists do. But it's important to remember that breakthroughs come with necessary costs, including vulnerability, fear, and emotional dysregulation.

When a client feels exposed, without enough grounding, they may be at greater risk of relapse or therapeutic ruptures. Trust, as we have talked about, is a moment-by-moment process, and a client who fully trusts you in one experience may start doubting everything that happens in the next.

Although insight is needed to make changes, insight alone does not lead to action. Sometimes there is a significant lag between developing insight and integrating it. This might explain why therapy often causes clients to initially feel worse about themselves. They have cultivated more awareness about themselves, but that awareness can be tremendously painful.

Furthermore, chasing breakthroughs can cause a sense of disillusionment in this work. Even when clients want to change, they are equally motivated to avoid change. When change does start happening, it is often on a granular level and with significant emotional upheaval along the way. If a client senses that they "owe you" a breakthrough, it can reinforce deceit patterns or people-pleasing behaviors to secure your approval.

So, what does this all mean? It means honoring the need to slow down. No relationship can or should be serious at all times. While therapy explores deep emotion, going full throttle without a break might backfire. Good therapy, like any trusting relationship, evolves, at different paces for different clients.

You may feel some pressure to "get heavy" or "go deep" in every session, but sometimes lightness carries as much weight as breakthroughs. Being a "caring, curious human" can be as important as being a skilled expert. Instead of only looking for massive changes, consider that lightness, humor, and play have merit.

Not only do the moments between strengthen rapport, but they also promote grounding and safety. You are still the therapist, and the client is still the client, but the humanness between the two of you feels more apparent.

Rest matters. Every hard workout, whether it's physical or emotional, requires an equally hard recovery. When examining the big moments, don't overlook all the depth that happens in between.

Guidelines for Honoring the Moments Between

- Remember that no relationship should be serious at all times. Muscles need time to repair. Emotions need time to settle. Clients need space for lightness, humor, and play.

- Don't inherently dismiss small talk at the beginning or end of the session as irrelevant. These interactions can be grounding for clients, and they help build and maintain rapport.

- Get to know your client's interests, preferences, and hobbies. Who are they outside of their presenting problems? How can you harness this information to connect with them in a way that instills hope and meaning?

- Remember that your authenticity can be incredibly connective for a client. If it feels appropriate to laugh out loud or make a silly comment, consider seeing how it lands. Your humanness can also help facilitate trust and safety.

- Honor that there are always good reasons for staying on the surface. Join your client there and make yourself comfortable with them. Taking the pressure off (for both of you) is an important part of conveying respect and meeting the client where they are at this moment in time.

SIGNS THERAPEUTIC IMPACT MAY BE OCCURRING

We end this chapter by answering the question, *But how do I know if I'm helping my clients? Am I actually having an impact on them?*

The short answer is, it depends, and there's no foolproof way to know. The long answer is that you can reference some of the following cues to assess treatment efficacy. As with all things in therapy, not all guidelines apply to every client.

Stated therapeutic integration: We define therapeutic integration as the times when clients explicitly acknowledge incorporating material from therapy into their daily lives. A client might say, "I thought about what we talked about last week." Another client might tell you, "I tried journaling after you suggested it, and . . ." These statements convey clients' efforts to integrate treatment material into daily life and demonstrate that they have *some* trust that what you offer may be helpful.

Direct praise and appreciation: Many clients will praise the therapy process with feedback like "That's a good question!" or "That's a great point—I didn't think of it that way." They may also directly thank you for how you have helped them. These explicit statements can all indicate potential therapeutic impact occurring.

Enhanced motivation: Therapeutic impact can also come in the form of direct behavioral change. A client may start building more momentum in their treatment and begin inching closer toward achieving their treatment goals.

Mirroring and parroting: Just as therapists mirror clients, clients can mirror us. Impact sometimes comes in the form of adopting your language, mannerisms, and rhythms in therapy. A client might tell you, "So, I know what you're going to say," or they might start using some of your familiar catchphrases in sessions with you. This may confirm the consistency of your work and the impact it's had on your client.

Comments about trust and safety: Note comments that allude to the unfolding of trust or safety within the therapeutic relationship. These can include "It's good to get this off my chest" or "I really don't tell this to anyone" or "Thank you for listening to this." These acknowledgments may highlight your client's willingness to engage in more vulnerable discussions with you.

CHAPTER 7

WHAT IF YOU MAKE A
MISTAKE WITH A CLIENT?

The *R* in our CHAIR framework stands for *repair*, which is a therapist's ability to reconnect and reattune to a client after a misattunement or rupture. Such "misses" can occur in any therapy, and it is important for you to feel comfortable executing skills to repair them with your clients.

As mentioned, it is impossible to be fully in sync with another person at all times. Sometimes you make a poor judgment call; other times, you are simply a human participating in a sometimes messy and emotionally charged relationship.

Let's talk about misattunement first. If a client's feeling of misattunement on your part came with a script, it might say, *I sense you don't understand me.* It might also say, *Even though you're with me, I feel alone in this.*

Again, misattunement occurs in every dyad. You just can't fully understand someone's emotional state in each passing moment. Given this, we can conceptualize that most relationships follow a sequence of connection, disconnection, and reconnection. This sequence is neither good nor bad, and the goal can't be to avoid all forms of misattunement.

A rupture can happen when a misattunement is significant. If ruptures came with a script, they might say, *I sense I can't trust you at this moment.* Sometimes they could also say, *I didn't like that, and I don't like you.* When a rupture happens, the client's perception of safety and connection feels threatened.

Ruptures can happen quickly, subtly, and insidiously, despite the therapist's best intentions. For example, maybe you forgot your client was recently fired from their job and you ask them how work is going. They now feel angry and hurt that you didn't remember this important detail they talked about in a previous session.

Maybe you told another client that you are pregnant. They smile and congratulate you, but they feel privately upset. They are worried about the possibility of needing to start treatment with someone else.

Sometimes ruptures are slight. You glance at the clock for a quick second, and the client observes your movement and thinks, *Oh, they're bored. They're just waiting for this to end. Why am I here? They don't care about this or me.*

Ruptures can sometimes organically correct themselves. For example, if you make a mistake, your client might naturally give you the benefit of the doubt without needing to address it further. But when that safeguard fails, active repair work becomes necessary.

RUPTURE, REPAIR, REPEAT

Psychologists Jeremy Safran and John Muran, who have studied the concept of therapeutic ruptures extensively, define a rupture as a "deterioration in the quality of the relationship between patient and therapist." They further divide ruptures into two categories: withdrawal and confrontation.[1]

Withdrawal ruptures are similar to avoidance strategies on the client's part. This rupture can come in many forms, but it entails a client passively distancing themselves from therapy or you. How does this show up in session? Your client could abruptly change the topic, start responding with vague answers, avoid eye contact, or become suddenly sarcastic. They may present as disengaged or disconnected when talking to you. They might cancel sessions or show up late. Withdrawal ruptures can lead to ongoing distancing behaviors. Sometimes this leads to a symptom relapse (even if you aren't aware of it) or premature termination.

Confrontation ruptures are more explicit. The client actively addresses their discomfort, dissatisfaction, or disappointment. They might, for example, tell you they disagree with your interpretation, and then they might criticize you for suggesting it. They could vent about how therapy is taking too long and muse aloud about your competence. Amid the tension, they might also accuse you of not caring or only wanting their money. In more serious forms, confrontation ruptures can lead to clients becoming hostile.

Many therapists feel uncomfortable even thinking about ruptures. We don't know anybody who's in this line of work *wanting* to hurt people, especially vulnerable people seeking help. Clients come to therapy seeking emotional relief—no therapist wants to trigger more agony.

But here's an important piece of data to consider. Research suggests that clients who experience positive rupture-repair cycles yield better treatment outcomes than clients who consistently have a strong alliance with their therapist.[2] It's worth soaking that in for a moment. You were probably taught that maintaining a strong alliance is one of the most important parts of effective therapy. But the ability to successfully reconnect with your clients when the alliance is jeopardized or weakened may be even more vital. Ruptures may be inevitable, but your commitment to repair them may be what solidifies a meaningful therapeutic experience.

A repair refers to a therapist's deliberate action to reconnect in response to a moment of disconnect. At a minimum, it is a genuine acknowledgment that *you* did something that negatively affected your client. Simply modeling this accountability can be profound. It's no secret that most people have limited experience with healthy conflict resolution in daily life. When you demonstrate a desire to repair ruptures, you're showing that you care about your client's needs and feelings. You're also conveying your ability to maintain unwavering compassion even if tension occurs. This may offer a corrective emotional experience, which can be paramount for clients with histories of relational trauma or emotional abuse.

In chapter 4, we highlighted the concept of supershrinks, which refers to a small sample of highly effective therapists. As you may recall, on average, despite their expertise, they receive plenty of negative feedback about their work. Some of their professional success may be contingent on how well they receive and integrate this feedback.

Effective therapy isn't about feeling connected at all times. But the rupture-repair process allows you to get it right when you've done something wrong.

IDENTIFYING RUPTURES

So, how do you detect a potential rupture in the first place? Researchers Safran, Crocker, McMain, and Murray have identified seven markers to consider in your work with clients.[3] We'll use a fictionalized teenage client, Taylor, to illustrate the many different shapes a rupture can take.

Let's say you have been working with sixteen-year-old Taylor for a few months. He was referred to you after being placed on academic probation for poor grades and defiant behavior in the classroom. You have been working on helping him regulate his emotions, build healthy study habits, and develop a sense of hope for the future.

One day, Taylor comes into session angry at his father, stating, "He never understands me. He doesn't care about me at all." You validate his feelings and ask if he'd like to talk more about what happened.

Overt expression of negative sentiments: Taylor replies, "Not really. You don't even understand me either. You're just paid to pretend to care." This is an example of an overt expression of negative sentiments, and this occurs when a client gives their therapist negative feedback via direct criticism or accusations about their competence.

Indirect communication of negative sentiments or hostility: Taylor replies, "Sure, whatever, I'll talk about it, and then I'll be all cured, right?" This kind of rupture often emerges through sarcasm or passive-aggression. It may be toward you or toward the treatment process itself.

Disagreement about the goals or task of therapy: Taylor says, "No, I don't want to talk about it. It's not relevant to anything we're supposed to be doing here." This type of rupture entails your client rejecting or disagreeing with particular treatment methods.

Compliance: Taylor shrugs and tells you, "Yes, we can do that." This type of marker can require a more sophisticated level of attunement. Clients sometimes comply with a therapist's request in order to please the therapist or avoid conflict. However, they may be privately upset or resentful.

Avoidance maneuvers: Taylor replies, "Nah, let's talk about this stupid shit I'm dealing with in math right now." Avoidance comes in the form of changing topics or declining to explore a specific issue further.

Nonresponsiveness to intervention: Taylor says, "Nah, I'm good. Talking about my dad is a waste of time. I feel like you should know this." This marker of a rupture may occur when a client rejects your intervention and does not agree that it's relevant.

Self-esteem–enhancing operations: Taylor shifts and says, "Sure, happy to talk about it. I'm failing practically all my classes, and it's because my dad is such an asshole." This type of rupture happens when clients offer justifications for their behavior as a way to defend themselves and potentially prove you wrong in a certain situation.

These markers are likely not all-encompassing, and we have found that they can blur into one another. In addition, noting a marker does not inherently mean that a significant rupture requiring complex repair has occurred.

Clients are entitled to their moments of frustration, confusion, and disconnect without it always being a serious therapeutic event. One moment of misattunement does not always lead to a rupture. A rupture happens when misattunement feels pronounced, leading a client to feel sharp emotions of anger, resentment, shame, anxiety, or humiliation.

However, therapists must pay attention to all of these markers. It is our job to track the alliance as well as we can.

Sharp attunement skills can help therapists note shifts in affect, which may indicate moments of tension. The desire to attune is how you respect your clients and prioritize the sacredness of the therapeutic relationship. We can't overstate the impact of the power differential that exists within therapy. With power comes responsibility. You must maintain a stance of humility, compassion, and empathy, and make an effort to connect as much as possible.

How do therapists successfully repair a rupture? Every theory will offer different approaches, but we will focus on the overarching takeaways here.

When managing ruptures, we often talk about the concept of being *deeply receptive*. This is an intentional word choice. Receptiveness comes in various depths, and we believe a therapist's job is to honor and step into that depth when the situation calls for it.

What does this mean, and how does it translate into your practice? Being deeply receptive means welcoming *all* reactions a client can have toward you. In the context of this chapter, we're focusing specifically on negative reactions. When these occur, you want to be *receptive* to the client's experience of what happened and their feelings about it. You want to understand how they interpret *you* and therapy at this moment, and you want to take the repair process seriously.

If Taylor were your client, and he told you, "You don't understand me either. You're just paid to pretend to care," you would have a wonderful chance to practice deep receptiveness. You might say, "I can imagine it's so frustrating to feel this misunderstood. I want you to know your feelings really do matter to me." Or, "I appreciate you sharing how you feel with me, Taylor. Even if you're questioning our work, I welcome that. It's okay."

Guidelines for Managing Confrontation Ruptures

Step 1: Identify whether a rupture may be occurring by assessing whether one of the seven markers occurred. Define whether the rupture is more rooted in withdrawal (the client withdrawing from you without addressing a problem) or confrontation (the client actively addressing a problem).

Step 2: If a confrontation rupture occurs, the first task is to remain *deeply receptive* and curious. Listen to your client's feedback closely and find the truth in what they're telling you. Remember that misattunement generally comes from a vulnerable place that might sound like *I sense that you don't understand me right now* or *I sense that you do understand me but don't care.*

Step 3: Keep in mind that your client may anticipate your reacting dismissively or defensively to their disclosure. You can defuse this by genuinely apologizing, thanking the client for their honesty, maintaining a consistently warm presence, and doing your best to stay attuned to their affect. Authenticity is imperative. It is never about proving a point; it is about trying to connect with your client's needs and pain.

Step 4: Prioritize reconnecting with your client. This can look like *How can I support you right now?* or *What might help you in this moment?* or *I'm so glad you told me this. How does this change things for us?* It is also powerful to say, *I'm so very sorry I hurt you.* Remember that you are on the same team, and if it feels like you're not on the same team, you need to consider how you can reconnect to that baseline.

Step 5: Consider checking back in with your client later in the session or the subsequent session. This can look like *I know we experienced some tension last week, and it's been on my mind, and I wanted to follow up on it with you.*

Guidelines for Managing Withdrawal Ruptures

Step 1: If you sense that tension may be present, do not assume you are overreacting or being sensitive. The tension may indicate your client withdrawing from you or reacting to something you said or did.

Step 2: Assess the tension by noting what shift (looking away from you, making a sarcastic comment, tightened body language, speaking shortly) occurred. Keep in mind that these shifts can be subtle and easily overlooked.

Step 3: Aim to make the implicit explicit. This sounds like *I noticed that you . . .* or *It seems like that struck something* or *I'm actually reflecting on what I just said and wondering if you disagree with any part of it.* Be willing to share what you observed with kindness and curiosity.

Step 4: Remain *deeply receptive* to any feedback your client provides you. If you don't understand any part of their feedback, seek clarification. Remember that therapy is about what ultimately benefits the client, and their feedback helps you orient your approach to meet their needs. Be willing to make reasonable accommodations if possible.

Step 5: Do not push a client to reveal some "big truth" to you. Respect clients for sharing what feels safe to them. They are entitled to individual feelings of ambivalence or frustration and may not want to openly discuss them at this moment in time. Hold the framework of CHAIR.

Step 6: If they do open up more, engage in collaborative repair by providing a genuine apology, holding space for your client's emotions, and asking them what they might need from you. Respect and validate the need for withdrawal as a form of preserving emotional safety.

More Considerations for Repair

- Remember that you and your client are a team working on the puzzle together. If, at any point, you no longer feel like you're playing on the same team, it's imperative to consider what might have happened. It's even more imperative to be willing to address it.

- Understand that clients might hesitate to offer you direct feedback. They might worry about upsetting you or your reacting negatively. If they detect even a hint of defensiveness, it could drive internalized shame, feelings of betrayal, embarrassment, deep anger, hopelessness, and questioning therapy or you as a therapist. This can result in various behaviors, including outward hostility, doubling down on compliance, avoiding the topic in the future, engaging in regressive behavior, canceling or skipping future appointments, and, of course, terminating therapy altogether.

- The repair process may include going back to the basics together. This can mean reviewing your initial treatment plan and revisiting therapeutic goals. These goals sometimes change, and a client must agree on the virtue of working on each goal. If they don't, there must be a collaborative effort about how to proceed. Just because you think a certain goal is important does not mean your client will agree with you.

- When an apology is in order, as it generally is in moments of tension, it should be genuine and offered with the intention to *connect*. Clients always have the right to feel angry, disheartened, and disconnected from their therapist. If you don't know what you did wrong, you can simply say, "I sense I did something that upset you" or "I want to take responsibility for saying/doing something that made you feel ___. That wasn't my intention, but I can see how it affected you."

- Sometimes the relationship in therapy mirrors that of past or current relationships. But do not assume that this parallel exists or overgeneralize that how a client might react to you is how they react to anyone else.

- Remember that the rupture-repair cycle can offer a corrective emotional experience, especially when clients have had limited experience with healthy conflict resolution. Many people come to therapy used to others becoming defensive or hostile when they make mistakes. Being able to offer something different can be healing.

WHEN YOU CAN'T SUCCESSFULLY REPAIR

Some therapeutic ruptures can't be remedied. Although this can be painful for everyone, it does not necessarily mean you or your client did something wrong.

Therapy sometimes harms clients, even when a therapist cares wholeheartedly about the work. Moments of significant misattunement or rupture might damage a client's welfare, and all therapists should be aware of this impact.

You have a delicate, relational-based role operating within a greater system. The system itself can affect this relationship.

For example, your client may disclose having the intent and means to complete suicide. Because you are a mandated reporter, you must breach confidentiality to protect your client's imminent safety. Your client feels both betrayed and enraged by your actions, and they discontinue treatment afterward. You feel guilty, and both you and your client experience a profound sadness over this rupture.

In another case, let's say your agency decides to raise fees for all clients. One of your clients can't afford this new rate, and they become upset with you, even though you don't control the finances. They end therapy abruptly and send you a long email criticizing your work.

These examples are distressing, but many therapists face them. Maybe nobody did anything wrong; maybe no emergency occurred that precipitated a no-show or late cancellation and they were charged for the session. But the chain of events led to a rupture that could not be resolved. This speaks to the extraordinary messiness that can occur within therapeutic relationships.

In other cases, clients will decide they don't like you or that they want to switch to another provider. They may sense that you don't have the competence to really help them. You may have said or done something they just can't get past. It happens, and while it can be upsetting, it is a universal feature of relationships.

Some relationships with clients will click in a way that others don't. Just as you aren't the ideal friend or partner to every person on the planet, you can't be the ideal therapist for every client who comes to your office.

Some ruptures can't be remedied, but you still want to wish the client well, keep their best interests in mind, and maintain professionalism at all times. Ultimately, a client does not need to "work it out" or forgive you if they have been hurt. It is our responsibility to honor their autonomy. Clients have the right to end therapy at any point—with or without an explanation.

CHAPTER 8

HOW DO YOU MAINTAIN COMPASSION AND RESPECT FOR YOUR CLIENTS?

"Compassion is the basis of morality."

—Arthur Schopenhauer, *The Basis of Morality*

S hould you have to treat people who have assaulted or murdered others? What about working with clients who hold hateful beliefs or taboo fantasies or act in ways that directly contradict your moral standards? What if they're blatantly sexist, racist, homophobic, or transphobic? How do you know what your role is when you feel disgusted or angry or upset by how a client lives their life?

All humans are unquestionably shaped by their values. No matter how much you try to embrace your open mind, some implicit biases are inescapable. Everyone has preconceived criteria for which behaviors feel acceptable or unacceptable.

Therapists work with people the rest of society often belittles, misunderstands, and ostracizes. When a client sees only the bad in themselves, you reach in and find all the good. You hold a light in a place that can feel so dark.

But what if you don't *like* the client? What if you not only disagree with their values but find their personality annoying or obnoxious? What if some or all of their mannerisms irritate or upset you? What if you find yourself feeling agitated during your work together?

Let's slow down here. We invite you to spend a moment thinking about a value you hate. *Hate* is a heavy word; we chose it because it triggers strong emotions. For example, maybe you hate self-centeredness or people acting like they know everything. Now imagine you have been assigned to work with a client who holds or embodies these specific traits. They show no interest in changing, but they're in a state of distress, they need help, and you have the expertise to help them.

Could you do the work? Could you genuinely support this client, find their goodness, and be on their team? In everything you do with them, could you commit to caring about their well-being?

Feelings of dislike exist on a large spectrum. Unfortunately, you may not be prepared to manage it when it happens. Negative countertransference arises when we experience conscious or unconscious negative reactions toward a client. Despite the word *negative*, these feelings are not good, bad, right, or wrong. But we must be mindful of how they can affect treatment.

Acting out as a result of negative countertransference can include:

- Rejecting your client
- Offering unsolicited advice
- Avoiding certain topics because they make you feel uncomfortable or unsafe
- Openly disapproving of your client's choices

- Withdrawing from emotional connection
- Being defensive or dismissive of your client's feedback
- Demonstrating inconsistent boundaries throughout treatment
- Trying to overcompensate for your dislike by being overly agreeable or passive
- Prematurely abandoning a client due to your own frustration or hostility

Negative countertransference sometimes happens when a client inadvertently knocks at unresolved parts of your own life. Maybe their anger reminds you of your father's anger, and you have a contentious relationship with him. Maybe their passivity speaks to your own difficulty asserting yourself, and you resent having to be the strong communicator in the relationship. Perhaps you're an unpaid intern and aren't sure if you can make rent this month and your wealthy client is lamenting about their next real estate venture. Because you are a human and not a robot, it would make sense if you felt agitated by these circumstances.

There are no bad clients. But some clients may feel bad for you. In addition to unpacking personal reactions in therapy and supervision, here are some guidelines for managing your emotions and offering helpful and ethical care to your clients. We explore them in more depth in the subsequent sections.

Leaning deeply into unconditional respect:
Deliberately choosing to respect your clients for who they are, where they are, and what they bring to you

Deliberately searching for the good: Intentionally

finding and holding on to your clients' strengths and virtues

Embracing empathy as a nonnegotiable: Prioritizing a warm, empathic approach with your clients regardless of your similarities or differences

LEANING DEEPLY INTO UNCONDITIONAL RESPECT

"People are just as wonderful as sunsets if you let them be. When I look at a sunset, I don't find myself saying, 'Soften the orange a bit on the right hand corner.' I don't try to control a sunset. I watch with awe as it unfolds."

—Carl Rogers, *A Way of Being*

Respecting clients means fully accepting them for who they are and where they came from. It entails honoring where they stand in their current journeys.

Respect moves into valuing autonomy. Clients have the right to live their own lives and make their own choices. You can have your opinion, but you do not live in your client's body, reside in their home or community, or manage their relationships.

Respect is the prerequisite for unconditional love. And love can be such a rich part of therapy, even if you don't identify with *loving* your clients in the specific sense of that word. Respect is also a catalyst for helping you release rigid expectations about how a client should think or behave. This opens deep space for curiosity and connection.

Respecting clients does not mean condoning problematic behavior. We're not advocating clients harming others or themselves. We absolutely want to see people make optimal choices in their lives.

However, respect means seeking to connect with the *context* and *motive* driving someone's behavior. As a species, each person's way of being is influenced by so many factors, including their culture, geography, upbringing, family influence, neurobiology, trauma, and genetics. It is especially important to remember this when working with clients you find challenging.

Respect can get muddled if you struggle with believing your clients owe you something. For example, therapists sometimes believe that clients owe them:

- Complete honesty
- A desire to do deep work
- The belief that therapy is a worthwhile investment
- Motivation for growth
- Insight into their current needs or problems
- A full understanding of therapeutic boundaries
- A willingness to integrate feedback
- Socially acceptable behavior
- Measurable progress

Having some parameters for treatment is reasonable. You are hired to support your clients to achieve specific mental health treatment goals. This work should adhere to certain protocols; deviating too far from the basic structure of therapy can create problems.

However, treatment in the real world does not exist in a predictable cut-and-paste formula. Clients come to therapy with unique personalities, unmet needs, and distinct behavioral patterns. Many arrive in a state of crisis when other resources have proven to be unreliable or unavailable. If they are mandated to therapy, they might resent having to meet with you altogether. In almost all cases, clients are juggling numerous stressors, and they want relief from their distress.

Respect helps therapists mitigate the risk of inappropriately generalizing or stereotyping clients. For example, let's say you conduct an intake with someone who discloses a horrible experience they had with another therapist in the past. They express their anger toward the healthcare system and tell you they have doubts that you can help them. Some therapists would flag this client for being "too difficult" or even "treatment resistant."

Respect means you give the client the benefit of the doubt. You listen to what they have to say about those past experiences. You care about their pain, and you *emphasize* that you care about that pain because you value their wellness.

As a therapist, respect means you hold the CHAIR (consistency, hope, attunement, impact, and repair) model as much as possible. You strive to convey a positively consistent presence for your clients. You find and hold on to hope for change in every way you can. You seek to attune to their emotions and needs. You look for opportunities to impact them and help them experience their world differently. And if and when conflict occurs, you take the lead in repairing that discourse.

Respect also means truly owning what lies in your locus of control. This, too, is covered by CHAIR. Ultimately, you can control the knowledge you obtain, the therapeutic actions you take, and the presence you exude. You control the boundaries you set, how you advocate on behalf of your clients, the referrals you provide, and the way you acknowledge making a mistake. Depending on your specific workplace setting, you may also control many logistics, including your fees, documentation protocol, after-hours contact, intake paperwork, and the arrangement of furniture in your office.

In reality, however, you can do everything you're clinically supposed to do, and you still can't control your client's reactions. You aren't in charge of deciding whether you have rapport. You can't fix whether a client's partner loves them or whether their boss perceives them to be incompetent. You can never control what a client does or does not do within the context of therapy itself.

The good news is that the more you can respect your clients, the more meaningful this work feels. This is because when you have a foundation of respect, you can lean more deeply into the *caring* part of this work.

We believe it's impossible to care too much about a client. To care is to be invested in someone's well-being. When you care, your heart and soul come into this work. It is one of the most beautiful traits you can bring to clients. As for us, we care about our clients immensely and wholeheartedly. We also have no qualms about telling them we care. We want them to know they are worthy of being cherished because they are. Holding this privilege gives our work such vitality.

Caring is not the same as enabling, overextending, or breaking therapeutic boundaries, however. Those specific actions often come from a place of caring, but they might speak more to unchecked countertransference, when therapists lose professional objectivity and presence.

Caring lends a hand to respect, allowing you to detach your compassion and tenderness from expectations. Within this state of respect, you genuinely want what feels best to your clients without defaulting to an assumption that you *know* what's best for them. You can value rapport and connection without ever demanding it. Most of all, you can and should care without conditions.

From this lens of respect, therapists can trust how the process of therapy organically unfolds. The freedom lies in the flexibility. It is the balance of accepting clients for exactly who they are while holding on to the hope that change can always happen. Therapy, from this framework, bursts with possibilities. Embracing radical curiosity sets the stage for holding unconditional positive regard for your clients.

You won't agree with or like every client you work with, but respect means trying to understand that most everyone is doing the best they can in a given situation. People want to secure their survival. Clients seek to avoid pain, even when that means hurting themselves or others.

How You Cultivate Deep Respect for Clients

Prioritize curiosity at its utmost capacity: What past circumstances led this client to make the choices they made? How, in every moment, are they seeking to minimize pain? Which behaviors have become solutions to temporarily cope with distress? Who hurt them and created those unhealed wounds in the first place? How are they trying to do the best they can with what they have?

Check in with yourself when you think a client owes you something: Be mindful of the tendency to assume your client inherently owes you something. If you find yourself struggling with this, ask yourself, *Why do I find this so important?* If you're struggling to let go of this expectation, practice saying to yourself, *How can I meet this client exactly where they are?*

Focus more on what you owe your clients: You owe consistency, hope, attunement, impact, and repair. You can't control how your clients respond to what you offer. Leaning into your locus of control may help release the demands you feel toward clients or the treatment itself.

Pay attention to your countertransference: Countertransference is not good, bad, right, or wrong. It exists and can't be avoided. But you can be mindful of how you orient treatment when it arises. Remember that your client, even if they remind you of someone or something you dislike, is a whole person with a distinct personality. Remind yourself often of this aspect of therapy.

Commit to neutralizing your values within therapy: In your personal life, you are entitled to orient yourself in ways that honor your values. But your job as a therapist is to show up and support your clients with respect, compassion, and professionalism.

Allow yourself to care tremendously: You are allowed to care about your clients. You are allowed to have feelings of protectiveness, adoration, warmth, delight, and closeness with the people you work with. Deep care, of course, should not justify consistently breaking therapeutic boundaries.

Have a plan if you simply cannot set your negative reactions aside: Sometimes this happens. You may not be able to work with certain clients because their content is too triggering to you. This does not make you a bad therapist. However, it's in your client's best ethical interests to refer them to a provider who can competently treat them. If this isn't possible, focus on getting quality supervision, consultation, and/or personal therapy to address your issues.

DELIBERATELY SEARCHING FOR THE GOOD

As therapists, we are called to search for the good, even when the good feels buried or insignificant compared with other traits we see in our clients.

It is also imperative to remember that no value is unanimous. As the philosopher Friedrich Nietzsche said in his book *Beyond Good and Evil*, "There is no such thing as moral phenomena, but only a moral interpretation of phenomena."[1] *Humans* have decided on some parameters of good and evil, but a choice that feels boundlessly immoral to one person may be entirely warranted to someone else.

If you assume a stance of moral superiority, you risk operating from a "me-versus-you" mindset. This mindset can create competition, and competition erodes the fabric of the relationship you're trying to build. If you aren't on the same team, you unknowingly risk becoming opponents. You may feel irritated, offended, and riled by your client. Your client may feel judged, condescended to, or unsupported. You both are apt to move into defense stances—and this defensiveness may prevent the crucial scaffolding of emotional intimacy from developing.

Your work as a therapist means signing up to care about people who think and act differently than you do. Biases are inevitable, but you must be able to examine inward and dismantle feelings of superiority. You are not a savior. You are not the all-knowing expert. You have simply been invited into a sliver of your client's life. You owe it to them to witness their pain and understand the gravity of their life story.

Searching for the good means assuming a stance of giving clients the benefit of the doubt. This becomes especially important when working with clients who feel challenging. When you can pause and drop into a client's pain, when you can land into the rawest feelings and deepest wounds, you soften. There are many ways for therapists to soften, but it happens when the therapist can truly land and sit with someone else's emotions, no matter how big, heavy, or confusing they are.

Softening is the catalyst for opening. Opening emotion, opening trust, and opening connection. Everyone needs a soft place to land, and you have the opportunity to create this place for your clients. Not all will take you up on it. But many will.

Your expertise isn't what makes therapy meaningful. Your courage to move beyond societal constraints and *listen* to another person is part of your impact. It's a deliberate choice. But in our judgmental world, you are privileged to get to make this choice every session.

It is tempting to find out what is wrong with your clients. The reward of this work comes from uncovering what is wholly good.

Embracing Empathy as a Nonnegotiable

Empathy refers to the capacity for relating and sharing feelings with another person. It means being able to sense what someone might be experiencing and hold space for that experience. When someone feels empathic, they feel warm, and people tend to be drawn to the energy of warm people.

What person comes to mind when you think of the word *warmth*? It may or may not be a therapist, but it's certainly someone who feels highly approachable and friendly.

Those who exude warmth demonstrate how much they care about people, and this care is felt through their words and actions. They tend to be optimistic without being overly positive. They remember details and they understand pain. They know how to hold emotions without overreacting or underreacting. You want to be around them because they feel safe, and that safety feels good.

Some people mistake empathic therapists for naive therapists. This, however, is rarely the case. Truly holding empathy without constraints means understanding and making space for all the mistrust, skepticism, and shame that people who walk into therapy carry.

Instead of condemning or withdrawing from those barriers, empathic therapists simply make space without any pressure or judgment. They respect the client's defenses for their necessary function. Empathy is patient, and empathy doesn't have an agenda.

We encourage therapists to self-assess their empathy by ranking themselves on a scale from 1 to 5 for each of the statements listed below:

1 = almost never
2 = rarely
3 = sometimes
4 = often
5 = almost always

- I seek to understand a client's pain deeply.
- I consider the context of why someone might think or act in a certain way.
- I can imagine what life feels like in my client's shoes.
- I am told I am a great listener.
- I am told I am warm or kind.
- I consider myself to be exceptionally compassionate.
- When I think about my most difficult clients, I

would rank myself as having an extraordinary
amount of empathy for them.
- I do not expect people to change on my behalf.
- I am patient with relapses, regressions, and setbacks.
- I believe I can genuinely sit with another person's
emotions well.

You want to strive for a score of forty or higher. If it's lower
than that, consider deliberately practicing more empathy in
your work or asking for help if you are struggling with a
particularly challenging client. Like any muscle, our capacity
for empathy needs to be worked out regularly to build
strength. But the stronger it is, the more you will connect with
your clients and respect them for exactly who they are.

Guidelines for Softening and Finding the Good

Imagine your client's younger self: Your client's present self
is a product of millions of interactions and experiences. The
"challenging" clients are often the ones who have
experienced extreme hardship earlier in their lives. When you
can drop into noticing their younger state, you will likely find
it easier to hold empathy. For instance, instead of solely
seeing a client as an angry, self-righteous man, you can also
see the part of him who is a fearful and helpless little boy.

Look past diagnoses and symptoms: Diagnoses are *theories*
that summarize a given set of presenting behaviors. Even if
you accept a diagnosis, everything is subject to scrutiny and
change as humanity evolves. It is imperative to push past
limiting thoughts such as believing that someone with panic
disorder or someone with schizophrenia automatically

170 FOR THE LOVE OF THERAPY

behaves a certain way. Diagnosing can be a helpful starting point, a tool, but it is never an end point. It does not paint the full picture of who someone is, what they struggle with, and what they need to move forward.

Practice more mindfulness: Slow down in session. Be more deliberate with how you listen and understand your client. If it's helpful, consider entering a potentially challenging session with the intention, *I will look for what's wonderful in this person.* When this notion is your compass, you seek to find strength and goodness.

Remember, everyone is trying to survive: This stance can't be emphasized enough. Recognizing this truth is not the same as condoning any specific behavior. Rather, it offers an understanding of why people develop certain patterns, no matter how destructive.

Prioritize empathy: Although empathy is often taught as a preliminary skill in graduate school, it's not a pervasive trait among all therapists. If you struggle with experiencing or manifesting empathy, focus on what might be in the way and, over time, prioritize implementing more empathy in your work.

PART III

REIGNITING YOUR LOVE AND PURPOSE AS A THERAPIST

CHAPTER 9

HOW CAN YOU BE A THERAPIST WHEN YOU'RE STRUGGLING IN YOUR OWN LIFE?

I n part I, we identified numerous barriers impacting therapist competence and confidence and examined why this happens. In part II, we highlighted how you can feel more empowered in the work you do with your clients, regardless of your current title or level of experience.

Now, in part III, we move into unpacking some day-to-day stressors, both structural and individual, that affect so many therapists in modern society, and we highlight numerous external factors causing therapists to question their work. We also provide takeaways and solutions that we hope can help you move forward.

In addition to questioning your inner qualities and your presence as a therapist, it's also typical to struggle with more existential concerns. Have you ever asked yourself any of the following questions? *How do I take care of others if I'm struggling to take care of myself? What if my own life is falling apart? What's the point of therapy when the world feels like it's completely ending?*

It is disturbingly easy to believe that the world is doomed. People are perpetually and mercilessly at war with one another. The earth's temperature continues to rise. Natural disasters continue to wreak destruction. Artificial intelligence is eliminating jobs and threatening every industry. Even when life feels calm, the curated algorithms provided by online media display infinite streams of bad news. With just a quick scroll, it's possible to access coverage of any crime committed in any corner of the world.

Sometimes the world feels like it's on fire. Sometimes it literally is.

Maybe you're in a crisis that's less about the world at large and more about you in your own life. Perhaps your spouse is acting distant or your mother has been diagnosed with cancer or you're worried about your worsening mental health. Perhaps you're dealing with death, divorce, miscarriage, bankruptcy, an affair, or personal illness.

These challenges are real and painful and exhausting. And the older we get, the more we experience the tragedy and loss that come with longevity.

Every therapist will experience a personal crisis at some point. It is only a matter of when, and it is not indicative of a moral failing. Everyone can relate to the feelings of agonizing sadness and red-hot anger and tight knots of shame. But while you may flow with empathy when your clients grapple with these emotions, reconciling your own can feel more challenging.

To complicate issues, many in our field unwittingly pathologize how we deal with our own adversities. Some therapists argue that it's never ethically responsible to treat others during a crisis of one's own. This sentiment may have some merit, but we'd like to hold a mirror to the shame that such rigid messaging can impose.

Let's say you experience a devastating death of a loved one. The sharpness of your grief feels as if it's splintered you into a thousand pieces. You oscillate among feelings of numbness, anger, and hopelessness. The heaviness is striking and undeniable, and everything, including your work, seems utterly meaningless.

Maybe it feels as if you can barely show up for yourself. How are you supposed to also show up for your clients? Are you even supposed to do that?

When a crisis occurs, concerned colleagues will likely recommend that you take time off to take care of yourself. This is an excellent starting point. While an absence from work doesn't take away the pain, tending to your own needs is paramount for healing.

But there's a catch. It is *ignorantly* shortsighted to assume that taking a break is the only solution or even the right one. First, few personal crises are ever resolved by taking just a few days or weeks away from clients. In many cases, even if you're not at work, you must manage other logistical matters that make it hard to fully replenish yourself.

Are we saying, then, that you shouldn't take time off? No. Of course, it's a good idea to focus on your own emotions and engage in self-care, but not everyone has that option— perhaps, like many professionals, you don't have adequate bereavement leave or the financial wherewithal to take time off work. Now you're left *still* managing your feelings while trying to get through the workday. You may also feel guilty that you're not giving enough to your clients due to your own pressing emotions.

That's why it's never as easy as saying, "Take some time for yourself."

Some therapists welcome work as a cherished refuge during hard times. Distraction can be an elastic coping mechanism. Compartmentalizing during a heightened state may offer you momentum to move through distress without collapsing. If work helps you hold your footing by offering a routine, that's worth acknowledging. When your life feels like it's crumbling, it's important to hold on to stability in whatever form that takes. Ultimately, it's up to you to work toward a delicate balance that works best for you both personally and professionally.

TAKEAWAYS FOR TAKING CARE OF YOURSELF

There is no optimal way to cope with a challenging situation. But here are some suggestions that may help if and when your life feels like it's in shambles.

Label what's happening: If circumstances feel serious or destabilizing, start by validating your truth. Crises leave a deep imprint on the mind and body. Sometimes this allostatic load can feel excruciating—you have permission to acknowledge the emotional and physical gravity of carrying such weight, or, as psychiatrist Dan Siegel says, "Name it to tame it." Identifying your emotions offers you the chance to add some space between you and your reactions. It can cultivate a sense of mindfulness associated with your experience.

Welcome the emotions associated with your crisis: This can be hard, as most of us want to avoid, deny, intellectualize, judge, or push through our feelings. But holding back from the fullness of your internal experiences creates a sense of disconnection. This can amplify fear and maintain a sense of unworthiness. "Radical acceptance" is part of welcoming your emotions. It is a deliberate choice that doesn't stop pain but may help disrupt additional suffering. This notion is rooted in the concept that *attaching* to pain creates more distress than the pain itself.

Try the sacred pause: In her work, Tara Brach, psychologist and author of *Radical Acceptance*, advises people to pause when intense emotions arise. You can do this by trying to pause without acting or judging. The tendency to run or ruminate is common, but embracing the *sacred pause* allows fuller engagement and processing. Although it may seem paradoxical, pausing to notice how you feel or what you think can help you achieve a deeper sense of grounding. This entails choosing to accept life as a conscious, moment-by-moment unfolding. It is in this slow, mindful experience that a sense of safety can present itself.

Dial in the basics of your routine: Self-care doesn't remove the heavy load, but prioritizing physical and emotional wellness can shift some of the heaviness. Focus on implementing these basic additions to your daily routine: Breathe slowly and deeply whenever you remember to do it. Don't go too long without eating. Find sunlight and get outside. Set your phone to "do not disturb" and go to sleep. If a certain kind of distraction helps you laugh, lean on that. If a particular friend helps you feel extra loved, lean on them. Always lean on love. Allow yourself to move through one day or one hour at a time. Every small action of self-kindness has a cumulative effect.

Remember that being a good therapist is never contingent on having optimal life circumstances: Many remarkable providers either have overcome or are currently managing intense adversities. All of us need to try to hold ourselves as tenderly as the clients we treat—in good times, hard times, and all the times in between. We know this is infinitely easier said than done, but this is truly part of what it means for therapists to practice what they preach.

PERSONAL THERAPY

We'd be hard-pressed to find a successful therapist who didn't attribute at least some of their professional identity to the personal growth achieved in their own therapy. Your therapist is a personal ally walking alongside you in this emotionally taxing, vulnerable work. You spend your workdays giving space and holding space for others. It is so healing to connect with someone who can offer you unconditional support without expecting anything in return.

Professional benefits: Being a client offers an authentic perspective on the nitty-gritty process of receiving therapy. This is an irreplaceable opportunity. Only in this role can you feel the unsteadiness of transference or the discomfort of being vulnerable when sharing a sensitive story. You have to be a client to know what genuine rapport does or doesn't feel like. There is no textbook or professional training that can mimic this first-person take.

Undergoing personal therapy is, by far, one of the most valuable investments you can ever make to enhance your professional presence. If you have firsthand experience of *knowing* how challenging change feels, you have greater understanding and empathy when clients struggle to make such changes.

Personal benefits: The work in therapy offers a haven for processing your most tender issues. It doesn't matter if you know, intellectually, the skills or protocols to "fix yourself."

That knowledge does not inherently resolve your own depression or marital stress. Having insight into certain interventions does not inherently lead to healing.

What a good therapist offers you is a dynamic *relationship*. This relationship provides the container for unconditional positive regard, support, attunement, presence, and collaboration. In this space, you get to be yourself. You get to have your unsettling emotions and complex needs. And through that experience, you have the opportunity to heal.

While therapy isn't your only option for introspection and wellness, we believe therapists should be willing to invest in the very service they want their clients to invest in.

Finding Your Own Therapist

Unfortunately, therapists often face multiple barriers when looking for a provider. Nicole posted a meme on her @psychotherapymemes page that read, *A mildly hot take is that therapy for therapists is supremely important AND it can be very hard, expensive, and inaccessible for therapists to get their own therapy.*

She posted a poll asking how many therapists related to struggling to find a therapist for themselves, and 16,280 therapists responded. Some 48% of respondents stated that they were currently facing this issue; 36% said they had faced it in the past. To combine these figures, 84% of therapists in that sampling found it difficult to find their therapist.

There are many obstacles associated with finding treatment. Some of them are the same obstacles your clients experience.

The cost is a big one. One of the most "liked" comments on

that original post read, "As a therapist, I can't even afford my own services." Treatment requires time and money, and many clinicians are notoriously limited in both these resources. You very well may be charging a rate you could not afford to pay.

It's also typical to worry about privacy and confidentiality when it comes to your professional identity. In addition, many therapists, like clients, have experienced adverse or even harmful treatment in the past. For example, maybe a therapist disregarded your values or kept interrupting you when you spoke. Perhaps they initiated a dual relationship. Unfortunately, these negative experiences happen to ordinary clients, and they also happen to therapists seeking their own therapy. If you've been hurt, it makes sense to feel skeptical.

Finally, therapy can just feel uncomfortable! Part of you may want to dive into some of your issues, but another part may feel apprehensive. It can be scary to confront your pain or acknowledge the need to change certain behaviors.

Do we think therapy is necessary for therapists at all times? Not necessarily. Context matters, but we believe it's useful to reiterate the value.

Effective therapy can help you cultivate greater self-awareness, heal difficult experiences from your past, and better orient your future. It may also improve your self-esteem and augment the quality of your interpersonal relationships. If you're struggling with burnout or other logistical concerns within this career, therapy may offer you the validation or guidance you need to navigate this challenging time.

Getting the Most from Your Therapy

We've listed below some key ideas to consider when you are looking for a therapist:

- Determine any significant priorities before you begin your search. Doing so will narrow down options and increase the likelihood of finding someone who is a good match. Know that you are allowed to have nonnegotiable preferences in your therapy.

- Consider all the relevant options for finding a therapist, including tapping into in-network providers through your health insurance and local counseling centers. If cost is a concern, ask providers if they offer a sliding scale for fellow therapists. Many therapists do. Even if they don't, they may have referrals to providers who can help you.

- If you've struggled to find a good therapist for yourself, consider looking for a provider who specializes in treating therapists. These providers understand how to hold space for therapist-clients without getting intimidated or sidetracked by the client's professional role. Many will advertise their specialty on their websites. You can also look through various directories, as some therapists will indicate that they work with other therapists. The Therapy for Therapists Collective is a fantastic resource that offers a pro bono exchange program —you can receive free therapy if you opt to provide free therapy for another community member.

- Trust your intuition. Your therapy should feel safe and validating; it should not resemble supervision or consultation, and even if you discuss work-related issues, it should not feel like you're simply "talking shop" with a colleague. Although you may share career experiences, your therapy time is about processing and improving your personal life circumstances. Being a therapist is part of your identity, but it is not your entire existence.

- Let yourself be the client. This is your space to practice *receiving*. In this role, you get to receive insight and validation, and you get to let your therapist hold the container.

CHAPTER 10

WHAT IF YOU'RE BURNT OUT?

Employee turnover represents a significant problem in many clinical settings. It's no secret that a large number of therapists experience financial strain, limited support, and exorbitant work demands in certain roles. Some therapists leave their jobs or the field altogether. Others stick it out, potentially slogging through fatigue, resentment, and apathy.

As we wrote and refined this part of the book, we dove into research, but the real vigor came from our discussions and anecdotal findings with real-life therapists working in real-life settings. Burnout is everywhere. It's so prevalent that it feels like its own professional rite of passage.

In 2022, Nicole posted an open question box on Instagram asking, *Therapists, what do you question most about your career?* We then organized the nearly 11,000 responses into categories that included individual personality factors and a sense of competence as well as four overarching *external* categories, outlined below.

Many therapists find themselves questioning whether:

- They are burnt out (or if they *are* burnt out, what to do about it)
- They need to change jobs altogether
- They will ever make enough money to feel comfortable
- They even want to do this job

RECONCILING BURNOUT

Burnout is a discouraging topic to discuss, but it's essential to address. We feel we owe it to our readers to honestly acknowledge this pervasive issue and provide some gentle takeaways that may help. Every therapist has been warned about the perils of burnout, which refers to a chronic state of emotional exhaustion. Therapists can experience burnout at any point in their careers, and the symptoms can easily mimic depression or anxiety.

Burnout can also coincide with or exacerbate those mental health conditions. Burnout tends to emerge slowly, but the issue can feel parasitic, and its effects compound over time. One of the first signs of burnout tends to be increased cynicism toward clients or work tasks. This can result in a growing apathy—therapy starts feeling pointless or ineffective, or you notice that all your clients seem to "sound the same."

Some therapists note experiencing physical or emotional symptoms of somatic distress, sleep disturbances, persistent fatigue, irritability, numbness, and an ongoing sense of dread in everyday life. You may be coping with burnout if work feels arduous and long, and if it feels as if there's no real way out.

We are not sure whether burnout is entirely preventable in this career, at least on an individual level. Therapists encounter significant infrastructural issues, including low wages, demanding internship requirements, insufficient training, and enormous caseloads.

Furthermore, each therapy session requires emotional labor. No matter how dedicated you feel in this profession, you have a threshold for how much you can dutifully support your clients. When companies treat therapy like a commodity that can be served on an assembly line, as if providers can stack their clients right on top of one another, boundless problems arise.

Therapists can quickly become overwhelmed and resentful. They might start fantasizing about a new job or call in sick more readily. Exhausted, they may default to an autopilot stance where they show up minimally in session just to check the box of meeting with that client.

When this happens, both you and your clients can suffer. But even if you work in an optimal environment, the work of therapy still requires intense concentration, a committed sense of patience, and sitting with clients as they share the most harrowing parts of their lives. Some work days just feel heavy.

No matter how the emotions are sliced, occasional exhaustion may be inevitable. The natural reactions that can come with being a therapist can also lead to vicarious trauma, compassion fatigue, and imposter syndrome, which can drive burnout.

In *Sometimes Therapy Is Awkward*, Nicole delineated the differences between internal and external burnout, and we emphasize this distinction here. We define internal burnout as a personal state characterized by exhaustion, cynicism, and a reduced sense of internal accomplishment. External burnout is a personal state characterized by persistent external circumstances that impact professional functioning.[1]

INTERNAL BURNOUT	EXTERNAL BURNOUT
A personal state characterized by exhaustion, cynicism, and a reduced sense of internal accomplishment	A personal state characterized by persistent external circumstances that impact professional functioning
Most Common Causes • Unrealistic expectations to control client outcomes • People-pleasing tendencies • Lack of boundaries between professional and personal life • Lack of self-care • Problems/crises in your personal life that impact your emotional well-being • Specializing in high-risk populations	**Most Common Causes** • Toxic work environment • Strong clashing of personalities between you and your supervisor or other colleagues • Lack of or limited opportunity for workplace growth • Low wages • Jaded attitude about your company • Specializing in high-risk populations
Signs and Symptoms • Depressed mood • Strained interpersonal relationships • Perpetual existential crises • Increased avoidance behaviors • Anxiety • Questioning your career • Irritability • Apathy • Compassion fatigue • Boredom in sessions	**Signs and Symptoms** • Dreading work • Resentment toward your supervisor, director, or colleagues • Procrastinating on essential work tasks • Dreading sessions with clients • Loss of respect for the company • Taking more shortcuts in your work • Chronically feeling underappreciated or disrespected

Possible Solutions	Possible Solutions
• Seeking personal therapy	• Working with a new supervisor
• Reexamining and implementing more self-care	• Discussing your concerns with management
• Shifting more of a focus onto your physical well-being	• Changing roles within the company
• Pursuing different professional opportunities (attending trainings, reading new books)	• Seeking outside consultation or supervision
• Taking a break from your career	• Strengthening your relationships with colleagues
	• Leaving the company altogether

In the following section, we focus specifically on four strategies for managing internal burnout, namely, diversity of work, personal relationships, aligned self-care, and growth. The acronym for these strategies is DRAG, which we find fitting because burnout can be such a drag on your emotional and physical well-being.

D: Diversity of Work: Varying the type of work you do
R: Relationships: Nurturing both your professional and personal relationships
A: Aligned Self-Care: Attuning to the specific needs that each season of life requires
G: Growth-Oriented Mindset: Cultivating professional insight and expanding your skill set

DIVERSITY OF WORK

Adding more variety to your work can be an important safeguard for preventing burnout. It may also help reduce burnout if you're already there. Fortunately, this profession provides numerous opportunities for embracing diverse roles. In addition to (or instead of) providing therapy, you may be fit for:

- Teaching as an adjunct professor
- Supervising
- Managing clinical teams
- Conducting research
- Case management
- Utilization review
- Patient advocacy

Many therapists also earn income through various side gigs. We have many colleagues who pursue different ventures, including selling art on commission, refereeing youth sports, or managing real estate properties. Even if these pursuits are financially driven, shifting energy into something completely different from providing therapy can be rejuvenating.

In our own work, diversity has proven essential. Our professional roles extend beyond direct client care, as we offer different types of clinical services, including consulting, supervising, professional writing, and speaking. The variety keeps us feeling well-rounded and grounded and helps us maintain a sense of vigor when we sit in our therapist seats.

Of course, "side gig" culture has its problematic pressures. We do not endorse the idea that everyone needs to work extra hours or embody different roles just to manage burnout. Nonstop hustling can also lead to exhaustion.

It's perfectly okay if you just want one job doing one type of task. With that, we still recommend committing to a mindset of ongoing learning. As therapists, we should all strive to strengthen our professional knowledge throughout this career. Keep reading. Keep attending trainings. Keep trying to absorb what makes you feel rejuvenated and inspired with your clients.

If the work feels stale and the days are running into one another or the sessions feel blurry and mundane, it may be time to infuse diversity within your therapy practice itself. There are many ways to do this if you have choices at your workplace, including taking on new clients with different presenting issues, learning more about a different modality, switching supervisors, or taking an intriguing workshop. Exposing yourself to novelty can keep your career fresh. It can also increase your openness to growth and add a sense of passion, both of which can help with burnout.

RELATIONSHIPS

Who are you away from your office? Who are you as a friend, spouse, parent, adult child, neighbor, or volunteer? Which relationships give your life personal meaning? How do you choose to love fully, deeply, and wholeheartedly?

As a therapist, you spend your day holding intimate emotions. You engage in deep conversations and spend your time onboarding, conceptualizing, intervening, attuning, repairing, and terminating clients. To be in this work is to be in the professional business of making and maintaining relationships. You manage each client-therapist relationship, and no two client-therapist relationships are ever the same.

You can and should care deeply about the relationships you form with your clients. Sometimes you bring your whole self to work, absorbing each client's needs and emotions. This can be taxing. You might ruminate about a session long after it ends, questioning your interventions or worrying about what to do next.

At other times, staying present is challenging. The needs in your own life can affect how you sit with clients. When you feel triggered by your own emotions, this disjointed energy makes it harder to focus on work.

Do you lack an "off" switch at times when your professional identity commingles with your personal identity? If so, you may prefer defaulting to a helping role rather than asking for support yourself. Loved ones can reinforce this pattern by expecting you to emulate your role as the sensible therapist in all settings.

WORK COLLEAGUES

Isolation is one of the greatest detriments of this work. Most therapists work alone with their clients. You may spend your entire day without speaking to another colleague. If you work in private practice, you have to intentionally reach out to other professionals to connect.

Isolation can perpetuate loneliness and insecurity. It may also increase the risk of burnout. Although therapy is conducted privately, the process of learning, absorbing, and deconstructing its nuances requires social participation. This is why we must stay connected to supervisors and peers. Staying attached to professional support may help you feel more satisfied. It feels tremendously validating to connect with others who understand the rigors of being a therapist.

But peer support for the sake of *friendship* also matters. When we spoke to more experienced therapists, several of them referenced the benefits of having a "tight-knit group of colleagues" as their best safeguard against burnout. Colleagues offer connectivity, and connectivity can keep us feeling inspired and fulfilled in this challenging work.

The perk of workplace connectivity isn't unique to

therapists. The global analytics and advisory company Gallup has conducted numerous studies examining workplace relationships, productivity, and company morale with millions of employees around the world.

Gallup's recent research indicates that about 20% of employees have a workplace best friend, a percentage that has been steadily declining over the years. However, those 20% are seven times more likely to be engaged in their roles. They are also more likely to produce higher-quality work and experience greater levels of emotional well-being. To highlight this point, another statistic from Gallup found that people without workplace best friends had only a 1-in-12 chance of being engaged.[2]

PERSONAL RELATIONSHIPS

One of the saddest misconceptions in modern society, particularly in Western culture, is that people should experience a sense of being whole exclusively on their own. Autonomy matters. It has an essential role in emotional wellness. But humans are social creatures, and we are biologically driven to rely on others for survival and connection. It is important to find happiness within, but happiness is not solely an inside job.

Your capacity for giving, listening, and holding space represents some of the key ingredients underlying effective therapy. The connections you form with clients can feel immensely gratifying. But clients do not hold you in the ways all people need to be held. They cannot offer a dynamic for reciprocal vulnerability.

Who holds you when you stumble? Who validates you for the ardor of spending your day validating others? Where are you allowed to safely cry and be yourself and be a human with human needs?

Many colleagues of ours concur with the following statement: *I come home, and I don't want to talk or listen to anyone. I don't care about my spouse's problems, and I don't want to socialize with my friends. I've been talking and listening all day. I just want silence.* Others agree with this statement: *I am so exhausted by emotions that I don't want to feel anything at all.*

There must be space for solitude. It can be exhausting to be in the "listener" role for hours at a time. Therapists need to recharge and regroup as part of their self-care. But strict isolation or patterns of emotional withdrawal can strip us of our basic need for connection. And if you consistently pull away from loved ones or numb your emotions altogether, you risk perpetuating apathy and frustration at work.

At the other end of the spectrum, some therapists maintain their therapeutic roles in their personal lives. If this is you, you are a therapist everywhere you go. Your friends and family depend on you for advice or emotional support. You may find yourself nurturing and helping others even when you feel drained.

It's reasonable to default into the giving role; many therapists embraced this role long before they were professionally paid to do it. Your therapeutic skills can help you be a better partner, friend, parent, or whichever role you maintain. But the lopsided nature of only being the giver is shortsighted. You miss the joy and validation of others attuning to you. You miss the gift of *receiving* support when you need it.

When we talk about relationships as a way to manage self-care, we're talking about assessing how much love you have in your life. And when we're talking about love, we're speaking about it urgently. If food is what nourishes the body, connections are what nourish the soul. This applies to therapists as much as it applies to any human on this planet. Love matters, it has always mattered, and a lack of it can be crushing.

Relationship struggles are universal, but failing to prioritize love is both a personal and a professional detriment. It is through genuine love that we learn patience and compassion. It is where we experience our greatest joys and our most meaningful memories. It is what gives a purpose to life.

Self-love creates the initial framework for how you want people to treat you. Loving yourself deeply matters, but it will never satisfy the essential desire all people have to love and be loved by others. You were not meant to solely fend for yourself. Your literal survival is rooted in a biological need to attach, connect, and belong. And although relationships often become the origins of our deepest traumas, relationships also serve as the catalysts for our deepest healing.

Connection matters. Connection *has* to be prioritized.

How do you let yourself give and receive love? Can you allow yourself to land in your rawest state with other people? And if you have relational attachment wounds, as many people do, can you commit to working and healing those aches? Even if you're skeptical? Even if it terrifies you? Not just for your clients. Not just for your work. For you. For your life. For this one short gift of a ride.

ALIGNED SELF-CARE

Do you know anyone who was able to successfully treat their burnout by taking a three-day weekend? How about a one-week vacation? Or even a three-week one?

We don't. But we do know many people who thoroughly

enjoyed their vacation and felt angry when they returned to work. We also understand that many therapists can't relax when they take time off. They feel too preoccupied thinking about all that awaits them when they return.

Although we may be in the golden age of prescribing self-care to clients, this popular term has become frustratingly co-opted and commercialized. From drop-in yoga classes to aesthetically pleasing ice cream sundaes, nearly every industry tries to entice customers to pull out their credit cards with the idea of purchasing self-care. It's no longer about selling a needed product or service. It's about selling wellness, happiness, and self-worth. To buy self-care is to invest in *your* well-being, and why shouldn't you want to invest in your well-being?

Therapists have also jumped on the self-care bandwagon. Your client feels depressed? They need to dial up their self-care! Your client is more anxious than usual? Let's talk about self-care! Your client is experiencing grief? Don't forget self-care!

When therapists struggle at work, they are also reminded to diligently take their self-care medicine. Whether you feel insecure about working with a client or are on the cusp of burnout or can't stand your supervisor, you've probably been given the self-care prescription.

And so, there's a good chance you have tried to practice self-care in ways you see fit. Maybe you have set boundaries with your employer and taken walks during your lunch break. Perhaps you indulge in monthly massages, cuddle your dog regularly, or meditate for a few moments each night. Therapists with more money and resources can access self-care outlets more frequently; having financial security allows you to book restorative vacations, pay out of pocket for personal therapy, limit your hours at work, and simply spend more time doing what you enjoy.

But has self-care fixed your burnout?

Maybe. Probably not.

As noted, we have our gripes with the commodified modern self-care movement. For one, it's largely embedded in capitalistic ideals that are anchored in fierce autonomy. From this framework, wellness is an individual pursuit, and it should be pursued to the highest degree. The focus on individual welfare often coexists with a prevailing myth that doing *enough* self-care should resolve any particular struggle.

It can't. And although most people logically know this, societies and people can quickly blame individuals for their adversities. If you don't feel better despite practicing self-care, it's *your* fault. Something is wrong with *you*. You're not doing enough, and you really should try harder. If you feel disrespected at work, why aren't *you* setting better limits with your boss? If you feel depressed, why aren't *you* going for a jog instead of lying on the couch? If *you* took better care of yourself, you wouldn't be dealing with burnout.

It is possible that society has become so obsessed with the construct of self-care that self-care itself has become a futile measuring contest. From this more cynical point of view, it's no longer about people practicing self-kindness. Instead, it's about our society convincing people to think poorly about themselves for not taking care of themselves more. In some ways, the hyperfocus on individual welfare can distract people from scrutinizing the circumstances impacting prosperity and health in the first place. This world is never perfect, and while self-care can make the pain more bearable, it can't fully close that gap of discomfort.

These criticisms aren't intended to discount self-care as a whole. The concept holds extraordinary value. We are, in so many ways, responsible for looking after our own needs. Self-care can preserve emotional well-being, soothe the sharp edges of intense emotions, and make life feel more vibrant and meaningful. Practicing self-care helps people build healthier relationships with themselves, which can lead them to make better choices overall.

But someone can absolutely sleep well, eat nutritious foods, socialize with a loving group of friends and family, and still experience burnout. At the same time, it's worth noting that those symptoms may become worse if someone *doesn't* practice self-care.

WHY "WORK-LIFE BALANCE" ISN'T REALISTIC

So, amid this seemingly contradictory information, how do you practice self-care? First, we like dismantling the generic concept of *work-life balance*. Although the concept sounds enticing, it is woefully unrealistic.

The notion of balance implies that life is static, with an even distribution of weight. But steadiness never exists in our raw reality. Every moment presents infinite stimuli, and how you interpret and react to those stimuli will change based on infinite variables.

Work-life balance also seems to imply that work is the opposite of life, and that's not necessarily true. Work is a part of life. It does not need to be sequestered into its own hemisphere and detached from every other priority. So, while chasing this concept of balance can feel tempting, it's often more helpful to shift into *aligning* priorities.

Instead of perceiving balance as the way people structure their day-to-day routines, it can be grounding to remember that life moves in seasons, with varying needs of different intensities. Some seasons require you to prioritize your work, and other seasons call for more attention to family or physical health. There are times for grinding and occasionally overextending, and there are times for leisure, reflection, and indulgence.

Certain seasons feel like a mild spring, others feel mundane or even forgettable, and others are dramatic and metamorphic. The seasons themselves have variations. Winter can bring a sequence of sunny days, chilly days, and a week of snow. But these sequences matter in this stacking of life, and it is a blessing to lean into each season and its related priorities.

We like to define *aligned self-care* as the ability to attune to what you need at a given moment. Take, for example, having a free hour on a Sunday afternoon. Sometimes aligned self-care will look like spending that hour catching up on paperwork. Even if it doesn't feel ideal to make this choice, alignment comes from knowing that you value feeling prepared for work tomorrow. "Monday you" is depending on "Sunday you" to take care of this important need.

At other times, aligned self-care means spending that hour taking a nap. Your body is tired, and the alignment comes from knowing that you tend to your priorities above anything else at that moment.

Guidelines for Practicing Aligned Self-Care

- Get in the habit of asking yourself, *What do I really need right now?* You may note that, at times, what you sense you need clashes with what you want, but practice listening to what you need. DBT practitioners often talk about listening to the Wise Mind. The idea is that our rational mind uses logic and rationality to make decisions, and our emotional mind relies on emotion and core psychological needs. The Wise Mind quietly aims to blend both perspectives to better harness our intuition.

- If you still don't know what you need at this moment, ask yourself, *In twenty-four hours, what will I wish I had done for myself right now?* Orienting yourself to your future self may help you recognize what priorities most need to be tended to now.

- If you're engaging in self-care to "stop" feeling sad or anxious, you're likely holding yourself to unrealistic expectations. It's normal to want to avoid feeling uncomfortable, but "moving into" an emotion opens space for mindfulness, and mindfulness allows you to slow down and consider how best to lean into what you need. Self-care is a way to honor your well-being and prioritize your physical, emotional, interpersonal, and financial wellness. It's not about eliminating or suppressing certain emotions altogether.

- Many companies commodify wellness and act as if they know your body and soul's needs better than you do. This isn't to say you can't buy comfort or relief in the form of a lovely massage or favorite dessert. But self-care isn't always found in external indulgence. It often exists in quiet acts of self-love, deep breaths, long walks, good conversations with friends, or snuggling with your pet. You don't necessarily have to spend time, money, or emotional energy to rejuvenate yourself.

- Some seasons call for more grinding. During those busy times, your options for self-care may be more strained or limited. Self-compassion matters here; being perfectionistic in your quest toward practicing self-care is antithetical to benefiting from self-care.

- When in doubt, when you really don't know what to do or what you need, take several deep breaths and go outside for a few minutes. Feel the earth underneath your feet and remember that you are just a speck in this vast universe. This existential reminder can be quite grounding.

GROWTH-ORIENTED MINDSET

Lacking passion for this work can be one of the first signs of burnout. It can also become a chronic issue that affects your ability to treat clients effectively.

Like anything, passion isn't a fixed state. Instead, it waxes and wanes. Even a dream job can morph into a collection of frustrating tasks. If you feel like you've lost passion for being a therapist, it doesn't necessarily mean something bad has happened. However, you may need to take a more active stance to bring the vitality back into your role.

Having a growth-oriented mindset helps maintain and revitalize passion. Growth-oriented therapists strive to continually learn and develop themselves. They maintain momentum within their careers. They seek inspiration and want to improve their craft.

At first, this may seem paradoxical. You might think, *Doesn't all that learning and absorbing put me on a fast track to feeling burnt out? Shouldn't I just be able to slow down and enjoy the work?*

No. Stagnation and complacency are some of the main markers of burnout. Think about some of your most meaningful hobbies or relationships. What makes them fulfilling is the *active role* you play in cultivating them. There's intention in how you show up and stay present with these parts of your life. This, in turn, spurs a sense of connectivity. Feeling passion often comes down to *prioritizing* passion.

Outside of your clinical sessions, you can embrace having a more growth-oriented approach to your work by:

- Reading therapy-related books
- Listening to therapy-related podcasts
- Watching therapy-related videos
- Consuming therapy-related social media
- Being part of an active consultation group
- Attending a new training or workshop
- Being an active participant in your own therapy
- Supervising other therapists
- Teaching other therapists
- Going to therapy-related conferences and/or retreats
- Conducting, interpreting, or writing about research
- Creating therapy-related content (courses, books, social media graphics)
- Getting involved in advocacy or social justice work
- Networking with other therapists

These activities offer more than just strengthening competence or learning a specific professional skill. They can also be restorative and lead to your feeling even more passionate about your work. They can anchor you as to *why* you chose, and continue to choose, to work as a therapist.

Taking a fantastic training can unlock a different approach to intervening with your clients. The right consultation group provides space to connect with people who have tremendous wisdom to offer. These activities keep you feeling engaged in the hard work you do.

However, there's a threshold. Burnout can happen when you try to do it all, when you don't know how to separate your professional goals from your personal wellness. As much as you can enjoy this work, it should not consume your entire identity.

We talk more about navigating this challenge next.

THERAPY AS A JOB OR CAREER VERSUS A CALLING

Many therapists argue about how other therapists should perceive our profession. For example, do you resonate with being *called* to be a therapist? Can it be okay if this is just a job for you?

Amy Wrzesniewski and Jane Dutton published an influential paper titled "Crafting a Job: Revisioning Employees as Active Crafters of Their Work." They classified vocational orientations into three types: job, career, and calling.[3]

> **Job orientation:** Therapists who identify with a job orientation typically view their work as a means to an end. Their job provides them with the money needed to support their life. Work is a necessity, but it is not inherently passion-fueled or meaningful. These individuals have the least emotional connection to their jobs.
>
> If you perceive your work to be a job, you might approach the day with a mentality that sounds like *I'm working here*

because I need the money or the benefits. There's not much passion here, but I have to do it. However, if you came into significant money or another viable career opportunity presented itself, you probably wouldn't hesitate to leave your current position.

Career orientation: Therapists who see work as a career often feel connected to their profession and feel ambitious to succeed. They value growth and success, and they care about their professional reputation. There is a satisfaction associated with building mastery, and this can reinforce a natural drive to learn and grow.

If you view your role as a career, you might have a thought process that sounds like *I like my work, and I want more for myself. I want to keep deepening my work with clients. One day, I think I might want to become a supervisor or director. I hope to get certified and learn even more. The work of being a therapist excites me.*

Calling orientation: Therapists who feel called to this work perceive their roles as integral parts of their identity. Their work does not begin or end in the office. It is a fundamental part of who they are and what they value most in life. People who feel called to their professions generally find their labor meaningful, and they may be willing to sacrifice other priorities to ensure that they can give their most to work.

If work feels like a calling to you, you might agree by saying, *I feel immense pride for what I do, and I can't imagine doing much else. Even during the hard days, this is what I'm meant to do.*

The important takeaway is that no category of work orientation holds superiority over the others. Each category represents a legitimate approach to managing your professional life. But we'd like to push back on some of the prevailing beliefs about how a therapist's identity might fit into everyday life.

For one, there's a prevailing belief that the best therapists feel called to this work. Consequently, people often romanticize the concept of having a work calling. It often represents the enactment of lofty childhood dreams. And who doesn't want to feel wholly fulfilled by their profession? Who doesn't want to go to work and feel like that is exactly where they are supposed to be?

The advantage is that the therapists who feel called to this work feel a deep passion for providing therapy. There is a purpose behind what they do. They often long to give others what they either graciously received or frustratingly failed to receive.

However, we can't dismiss the downsides of feeling tethered to a calling. Sometimes a *calling* definition can be too rigid or narrow. If your current role doesn't feel completely aligned with what you feel called to do, work can feel unbearable. This may result in your chasing a "perfect" career that may not exist at this moment in your life. It may not exist at all!

The calling mentality can also lead to overextension. When work is the most important part of your life, you may struggle to set reasonable professional limits. Think of the entrepreneur who spends seventy hours a week building his business or the high-powered executive who loves what she does but never sees her family. These professionals may not be doing anything outwardly wrong, but even the greatest labor of love is still labor. Over time, you may find yourself being taken advantage of professionally. You might also struggle to have any real identity outside of work.

Research shows that people are more apt to accept lower compensation for jobs they consider to be meaningful. They may also overextend themselves at work and struggle to set reasonable boundaries around their professional limits.

Shifting from Having a Job to Having a Career

There is absolutely nothing wrong with you if you perceive your work as a job. But it can feel depressing and frustrating when clients represent only a paycheck to you.

Going through the motions makes time move painfully slowly, and it can heighten the risk of burnout. People might experience an uncanny, repetitive internal message that sounds like *Is this all life really is?*

If you want to infuse more meaning into your work, here are some practical steps:

- Embrace a daily gratitude practice for your work in which you note glimmers that occur each day. Cultivating this kind of appreciation gives your work more meaning.

- Commit to one area where you can grow professionally: learn a new theory, get certified in a specific type of therapy, or join a consultation group.

- Identify a skill you want to strengthen and measure how well you execute it during each session.

- Identify all the ways your work matters to you and your clients. Consider making a list of these reasons. There are no small or insignificant answers. Continually adding to this list may foster a stronger sense of appreciation for what you do.

- Consider whether you feel content or valued in your current role. You may feel like *it's just a job* if you don't care much about the work you're doing. If other types of therapist positions intrigue you, spend time reflecting on whether and when it may be possible to make a change.

Shifting from Having a Calling to Having a Career

It can be an extraordinary blessing to feel called to help others. There's such beauty in feeling deeply connected to what you do.

However, the steep costs of overidentifying with your role must also be acknowledged. Maybe you feel like you give too much to your work or you can't separate your professional role from your personal one. Perhaps you've allowed yourself to be taken advantage of because you find such rich meaning in what you do.

If you feel like you want to dial down the weight of "being a therapist," here are some considerations:

- Spend more time cultivating your outside interests, relationships, and needs. Who else are you besides a therapist? What people or activities might benefit from having more of your attention right now? Prioritize building a life that extends beyond what you offer professionally.

- Commit to setting at least one or two professional boundaries for yourself that honor the need to "turn off" work. You are not responsible for being a therapist twenty-four hours a day.

- Be mindful of the fallacy of believing that a perfect career exists. Every type of work has its drawbacks, and it's okay if you don't love every single aspect of what you do.

- Consider that work can be a socially acceptable distraction. Some therapists pour all their energy into their work to avoid unresolved issues in their personal lives. This is neither good nor bad, but ignoring this pattern may have negative effects on your relationships, physical health, and emotional well-being.

CHAPTER 11

SHOULD YOU QUIT YOUR JOB?

The problem with external burnout is that no amount of self-care or gratitude will fix it. When external factors lead to burnout, internal recovery work only goes so far. Practicing self-care, acknowledging burnout, and having a positive mindset matter. But where is the space to implement wellness strategies if you lack time to breathe and recharge during the day? Setting healthy work boundaries always has its merit, but what happens when the boss ignores those limits?

Therapists can't meditate themselves out of abusive environments. You might try to reframe your thoughts, continue to work hard, and look after your well-being. But again, individual efforts can't necessarily change negative or unscrupulous working conditions.

We want to talk about exploitation in the mental health industry because it exists everywhere. Many of the highest-stress jobs also come with the lowest amounts of compensation. If you are a trainee or intern, you may not be receiving any pay at all.

The trope of *paying your dues* is so mainstream that therapists are often told to *expect* harsh working conditions, low wages, and questionable clinical practices as "part of the process." There remains a widespread belief that clinicians need to grind to move up, and it continues to be reinforced as therapists take on exorbitant student loan debt and move through unpaid internships and low-paying jobs.

It is no wonder that so many therapists feel discouraged and overwhelmed. It is also no surprise that some of the most passionate providers leave the profession altogether. We know many therapists who emotionally love the work yet feel utterly crushed by the logistics of the work itself. They care about their clients, but they are assigned to work with too many people. They are implicitly and explicitly commanded to focus on outcomes and productivity over quality care. If they are brave enough to ask for more support, they're generally met with canned responses along the lines of *Do your best* or *This could be helpful to talk about in your own therapy* or, as we just referenced, *Make sure you practice self-care!*

We think it is important to propose some concrete criteria indicating a problematic clinical environment.

The following criteria don't stem from an exact science; they are based on our anecdotal experience, countless conversations with other clinical professionals, and research focused on organizational burnout:

- Routinely being asked to perform tasks outside of one's scope of competence
- Excessively high caseloads with limited to no time for breaks
- Inadequate compensation based on job role, experience, and cost of living
- High employee turnover rate

- Poor communication among staff and management
- Chronically being understaffed
- Disregard for employee work-life balance
- The company engaging in fraudulent, illicit, or immoral behavior

If your current role meets some or most of these criteria, you have good reason to feel concerned. While no job is perfect, in a healthy environment, you experience an ongoing sense of respect. Employers who respect their therapy staff understand the scope of practice and competence. They provide staff with appropriate resources, training, and support to do their jobs successfully. Workplace respect also entails honoring a therapist's personal needs, which include proper compensation, time for rest, and sincerely listening to their requests with curiosity. Above all, the employer is receptive to feedback. If you approach them with concerns, they listen to your feelings and collaborate with you to make reasonable accommodations.

Honest discussions about exploitation are missing in most therapy trainings and graduate programs. Most therapy books also don't cover this topic. Fortunately, we have witnessed this topic being called out on social media, and we're grateful.

To date, one of Nicole's most liked, commented, and shared posts reads: *Can we talk about how exploitative most internships are? Here are your 50+ clients, no compensation, a useless supervisor, and the a/c doesn't work. But be grateful and get your hours signed. It's time to kill this trend.* The popularity of this post speaks to the harmful working conditions so many therapists experience.

If this is your story, you deserve to be seen and validated. Failing to do this only perpetuates the ongoing phenomenon of therapists feeling unrepresented and unvalued. Since we respect the work of all therapists, we hold every organization to the highest standards of professional care. Just as clients have the unquestionable right to ethical treatment, their providers do as well.

It is demoralizing to feel exploited. How can you feel fulfilled as a therapist when your pay is dismal and the hours feel relentless? How do you give the most to your clients when you're supposed to see eight, nine, or ten of them every day? In many ways, you can't. You do your best, but you will always feel compromised.

So, what are you supposed to do if you're in this space right now?

Here's what we won't say: *just quit your job.*

If it were that easy, you probably would have already quit. Although we don't advocate exploitation, we also don't minimize the predicaments associated with leaving a job. Even if quitting is the best answer, it's rarely that straightforward. If it were simple for every therapist to leave a harmful work environment, those types of companies would either be forced to change or disappear altogether.

You might be working in your current role for many reasons. Client care, financial security, valuable benefits, convenience, relationships with coworkers, needing to obtain hours toward licensure, and liking some or even parts of the job are common motives. We have experienced every one of these variables at different points in our careers. The idea of leaving can also open immense fear. *What if I'm abandoning clients who need my support? What if there isn't a better job out there? What if I regret my choice after all?*

Any significant change comes with a sense of upheaval. We don't shame therapists for grappling with tough career decisions. Therapists, after all, are people trying to pay their rent, feed their families, and offer meaningful work to their clients.

In addition, their clients, many of whom can recognize the systemic dysfunction in treatment, often cite their therapists as the lifeboats amid the chaos. Those clients also deserve excellent treatment, even when the circumstances are not ideal.

LEAVING YOUR JOB

If you are on a path toward eventually leaving an exploitative position, we commend you. It may be helpful to share this: In all our conversations with therapists who left problematic roles, we did not encounter anyone who permanently regretted their choice. Many did share the uncertainty they felt just before and after leaving. Some spoke about the uneasy stumbling or second-guessing that occurred afterward. But not one person said, "It was a terrible choice. If I could, I'd go back."

If part of you feels ambivalent about what to do, we invite you to welcome any fears that you notice. No fear is too small, irrational, or insignificant. Fear doesn't just appear randomly either. Drop into the discomfort of fear to help you understand your perceptions of danger. This is not about reframing your anxiety or invalidating a real emotion. It's just about temporarily sitting with your discomfort and seeing what emerges.

You might notice physical sensations or visual images from either your past or present. You may automatically attach words or meanings to this discomfort. Maybe it says, *What if I can't find a better job?* or *What if I'm just being too dramatic?* Stay with what you experience for a moment. Allow yourself to imagine making the change without necessarily attaching a timeline or concrete plan to it. That's the first step. And just like in therapy, knowing that alternatives exist can instill a sense of hope, and that hope may be one of the first steps toward initiating change.

Although we do not work in exploitative positions anymore, we feel dedicated to doing our part to name and help challenge these systemic barriers. All therapists can choose to hold unethical companies accountable. When policies adversely impact mental health treatment, you can put on your fighting shoes and stand up for what you believe in.

Dues should not have to be paid. Grinning and bearing high caseloads and low compensation should not be the norm when working with the most intimate aspects of humanity. Therapists deserve respect and safe working conditions. You deserve to be valued for the hard work you provide each day.

As we mentioned, sometimes you can manage external burnout by changing supervisors, talking to management, or changing roles within the company. But if those strategies don't make a dent in how you feel, it may be time to reevaluate the job altogether. That might not mean quitting today or even tomorrow. But it means knowing that, ultimately, you deserve to work somewhere where you can thrive.

For those who *are* in those challenging work conditions, who are juggling those high caseloads, who are building their careers with the resources they have, and who don't have the privilege of having an optimal career at this moment in time, we see you. *And it can get better.*

A FRANK CONVERSATION ABOUT COMPENSATION

Are you being paid well? Maybe. But possibly not.

Therapists are consistently among the lowest-paid professionals who have an advanced education. As noted, many clinicians are saddled with student loan debt and work in tedious roles receiving paltry salaries. You may be working multiple jobs to stay afloat. You might be tempted to leave an enjoyable position because you can't afford to live on your current salary.

Our field collectively disagrees on many issues, but fewer topics are more contentious than money. Therapist communities are full of heated arguments about salary expectations, equitable group practice splits, hourly session rates, sliding scales, and cancellation fees. People charging rates lower than the market value risk being dismissed for cheapening their work or having fewer skills. Therapists with higher fees may be labeled as greedy and selfish.

Millions of therapy hours have been conducted on the backs of exploited interns and associates working toward licensure. High-paid therapists may seem out of touch with their lower-paid colleagues when they talk about never settling for less than one's professional worth. The reality is that money does drive people to leave the field, and that fact alone requires serious conversation.

In this section, we attempt to change the taboo narrative about money and therapy. Money dictates survival, and it shapes motivation, drives behavior, and crafts life-changing decisions. Therapists need to welcome an open dialogue about it.

It's not enough to say, *Pay the therapists more!* Compensation matters, but employers should never leverage more money to justify dismal working conditions. And, unfortunately, this problem exists in our field. The "better-paying" jobs often pay well because they demand so much of their employees.

Many therapists recommend pursuing private practice. This option has its merits, but it can't be the universal answer.

When it's your practice, you're responsible for all aspects of your business, and you absorb all the financial risk associated with slow referrals, cancellations, and no guaranteed paycheck. Failing to address these drawbacks is ignorant at best and incredibly privileged at worst.

The phrase "You don't get into this field for the money" is another problematic trope impacting every facet of a therapist's work, from the school they select to which certifications they pursue to whether they opt to panel with a particular insurance company. On a macro level, money shapes the practice of therapy by determining how and which treatments are accessible for clients at large.

MONEY AND PRIVILEGE

Another part of talking about money is addressing privilege. Privilege will affect how therapists perceive and shape their careers from the beginning. For example, a young therapist with wealthy parents eager to support their child's professional ambitions can approach their career differently than a divorced, middle-aged therapist with three children to feed. An able-bodied therapist who can endure working long hours with high caseloads has different advantages than the provider whose disability makes full-time work impossible. Additionally, racism, sexism, classism, ageism, and other oppressive factors contribute to known compensation divides. We see this in all industries, and mental health is not exempt from such discrimination.

The lack of clinician diversity has been a rampant problem among therapists. Many clinicians are white, female, and able-bodied. Although the gender gap is lower among therapists than among professionals in other disciplines (likely due to the field's being predominantly female-oriented), women working full-time still earn 84 cents to every dollar for a man, according to the Census Bureau.[1]

We could share more statistics, but the heart of the problem is this: every therapist has a story about the complications between work and money. Maybe you work multiple jobs to make ends meet. Maybe you feel trapped working for a quasi-unethical company because it pays well or offers enticing benefits. Maybe you keep sliding your rate down, even if you know you should be charging a higher amount.

No chapter in a book can repair systemic financial problems. It's unfortunate that most classes, trainings, or conversations fail to address them. Change starts with awareness, but awareness needs to lead to discussion, and discussion must move into action.

Of course, it feels gratifying to love what you do for a living. However, love does not pay for electricity and groceries. Money does matter, irrespective of how much you care about your clients and the work you provide them.

It is bold but important to say that therapists who feel compensated fairly for their work may even care more about it. They might experience less financial anxiety or less resentment toward their daily tasks, allowing them to settle deeper into meaningful work. They may have more financial freedom to pursue trainings that are meaningful to them. They might also have more cushion to take time off when they need rest or rejuvenation.

More Challenging Money Conversations

When is it okay to work for an employer who commits fraud or doesn't act in their clients' best interests? How much profit should a group practice owner set aside for themselves? When is it permissible for a therapist to raise rates when their clients are struggling financially? How should a therapist respond to the criticism that they care only because they are paid to care or that therapy itself is little more than a paid friendship? What even determines a reasonable salary?

Do you have objective answers to these questions? We don't.

The topic of money is convoluted, and it tugs at different emotions. If you genuinely think money doesn't affect how you work, we ask you to briefly imagine that you won the lottery right now. What would you do differently? Would you quit being a therapist? If not, what fundamental parts of your practice might change? This lottery exercise isn't about vision-casting your perfect imaginary life. It's about honestly recognizing that money shapes your values, and your values affect your professional goals. Individual context also can't be overstated—compensation that feels desirable to a therapist in one location may be insulting to another therapist living somewhere else.

So, how can we end this section on an uplifting note? In some ways, we can't. We acknowledge that money stress is a real and challenging problem in our profession. Like ending an impactful therapy session, it's not always realistic to wrap up each elaborate problem with a beautiful bow. And our goal isn't to make you feel good. Certainly, the answer isn't to point fingers at colleagues and shame them for their career choices. Therapists working in suboptimal conditions already tend to dislike their circumstances. Suggesting that people *just raise their fees* or *quit that toxic job* often feels dismissive. It is naive to recommend that people arbitrarily make significant changes without considering the context of their lives.

This is why we avoid the types of grandiose promises other books or influencers make about therapy, such as "How to

Make Six Figures in Three Months." Bold, universal claims sound enticing, but they lack nuance—life is never formulaic. If you are a new therapist, be careful of "gurus" trying to sell you a formula for monetary success. Even if their strategy worked well for them, that doesn't mean it will work for you. If following a predetermined set of guidelines guaranteed financial success for therapists, we wouldn't be seeing such deeply rooted monetary problems.

Let's continue validating the harrowing struggle around money in our work lives. For instance, as concerned and caring professionals ourselves, we try to prioritize giving back in different ways: through donating to charity, offering sliding scale and pay-what-you-can slots, providing free psychoeducation and trainings, and engaging in local and national mental health advocacy. We do this while knowing it's still not enough. It doesn't pay anyone's rent or change their salary. It is just the part we've chosen to play in a large system.

If you can also give back, what choices will you make? And how will you balance giving back while still honoring your financial wellness?

Hope matters, so we also hold on to hope that the tide will continue to change. We have so much hope that the newer generations of therapists will hold themselves to high financial standards and continue calling out injustice and exploitation when they see it—whether that's toward their clients or themselves. This is how change happens. One conversation at a time.

CHAPTER 12

WHAT'S IN IT FOR YOU?

The word *love* is the most intentional word in this book's title. That's because in this line of work, there's so much to be said about love.

Clients often come to therapy deeply lacking love. They don't love their partners. They don't love their careers. They don't love their bodies or parts of their personalities or the ways they cope with stress. They don't love their pasts or how their lives have unfolded.

We live in a world that's ravenous for love.

And yet.

Do you love being a therapist?

Maybe. But possibly not.

When we talk about loving this work, we have to address a few misconceptions. It's unrealistic to love every part of the job. No matter how much you enjoy *anything*, certain emotions like frustration, fear, or boredom still arise.

Throughout this book, we have referenced knowing that many therapists don't love their work. Some resent what they do. Some trudge through sessions, struggling to stay present, trying to suppress their heavy feelings of dread and exhaustion. Many balance high caseloads while feeling unsupported by management and misunderstood by society at large. Others keep asking themselves if they should quit the field altogether.

We wrote this book for *all* these therapists. We wrote it for everyone grappling with the day-to-day reality of providing this kind of work. This is for the invisible, underrepresented clinicians who *want* to feel more love for the work they do.

Up to now, we have sought to cover the many complex and compelling issues affecting therapists in their work. You may be finishing this book feeling more clarity in certain areas and more discomfort in others. Ultimately, we hope you feel both supported and impacted, like you might feel after a good therapy session.

We're going to end by talking about love. Because when you lead with love, it shows, and it shines, and it helps both you and your clients. So, if you're struggling with love—if you're lacking passion or even the basic motivation to show up for work tomorrow—we offer some final glimmers to add to your toolbox.

DEEPENING YOUR GRATITUDE

The Roman philosopher Cicero said, "Gratitude is not only the greatest of virtues, but the parent of all the others." How different would your life feel if you prioritized gratitude as the single most important virtue? How would your practice change if you flowed overwhelmingly with appreciation for your work?

In a world that incentivizes people to have more, want more, and be more, it feels rebellious to sit quietly and appreciate what already is. In many ways, gratitude is the brave choice. It helps you disconnect from scarcity and resentment and lean into a mindset of abundance and love.

Of all the superpowers someone can possess, we are inclined to agree with Cicero. Gratitude sits either near or at the top.

Research supports these claims. Studies show that people with higher rates of gratitude are happier and more satisfied with their lives. They experience lower levels of stress, fewer symptoms of anxiety and depression, and fewer suicidal thoughts. They are more likely to be prosocial and give to others.[1] They're also more likely to engage in *upstream reciprocity*, which refers to helping someone else after being helped.[2]

If you regularly practice gratitude, you're more likely to be patient and practice delayed gratification. You may even have higher rates of resilience after traumatic events. One study found that breast cancer patients who experienced and expressed gratitude exhibited higher rates of post-traumatic growth, reduced stress, and more positive emotions.[3]

There's more. Gratitude is associated with numerous health benefits, including immune strength, improved sleep, and increased pain tolerance. Grateful people are less jealous and more optimistic about their lives. They tend to be more forgiving toward others. And when couples express and receive gratitude, the quality of their relationship strengthens.

If you're grateful at work, the benefits keep going. There's a relationship between gratitude and better performance. A grateful employee tends to be more satisfied with their work, and they are also more likely to engage in prosocial behaviors.[4]

One study found that when researchers asked teachers to count their blessings for eight weeks, those teachers reported better moods, more life satisfaction, a higher sense of accomplishment, and lower rates of emotional exhaustion. In another study, when healthcare practitioners (that's you!) wrote about work-related gratitude twice a week over four weeks, they had lower rates of stress and depression symptoms.[5]

We present this abundance of research because practicing gratitude is easy and free, and, as the studies show, *it works.* Therefore, implementing gratitude into your routine may be as essential as showering and brushing your teeth.

Still, gratitude is not a bandage for treating heavy emotional pain or glossing over the problems that may exist in your work. When difficult moments arise, gratitude allows you to stay more mindful and centered. It can also help you feel open-minded and kind.

Simple Gratitude Exercises

Naming three good things: Martin Seligman, the founder of positive psychology, recommends this exercise as a starting point for understanding and expressing gratitude. Intentionally reflect and write down three things that went well today. If you're struggling in your role, consider applying this exercise specifically to your work. Write down three highlights of your day and acknowledge *why* each specific item evokes a sense of gratitude.

Mental subtraction: Concentrate on what your life would be like if a positive event never happened. For example, you might visualize what it would be like had you never moved to a new city or met your partner. Imagining the absence of something you value can cultivate a deep appreciation for what you have. You can apply this to your work by thinking about what you value the most about your work (a certain client, your own office, a great boss, flexible hours) right now.

Now imagine not having those positives and how that would feel.

Collecting the highlights: Get in the habit of writing down the small and large victories you witness your clients achieving. You don't need to include any identifying information. Simply acknowledging, *Today, my client applied for a new job* or *My client was able to tell his partner what he needed* reminds you of all the wonderful changes that can happen as a result of your therapeutic work.

Death reflection: *Please note that this exercise may evoke intense, triggering emotions. We don't recommend doing it if you're currently in a heightened state of distress.* Vividly imagine yourself dying or think about the inevitable reality of death. Allow yourself to focus on the certainty of your demise. Research shows that people who have near-death experiences awaken with a dramatic and even urgent appreciation for life. Confronting yourself with the absolute end may help you feel grateful for this present, rare and fleeting moment in time. It may also reorient a pleasure in what it means to be alive.

REMEMBERING HOW YOU TRANSCEND CLIENTS

"We take pleasure not only in the growth of our patient but also in the ripple effect—the salutary influence our patients have upon those whom they touch in life."

—Irvin Yalom, *The Gift of Therapy: An Open Letter to a New Generation of Therapists and Their Patients*

In 1972, meteorologist Edward Lorenz wrote an article titled "Predictability: Does the Flap of a Butterfly's Wings in Brazil Set Off a Tornado in Texas?" In his research simulations, he found evidence showing how small errors within patterns multiplied quickly. An unpredictable movement in one region could affect what happens in another part of the world. To simplify, small changes could contribute to dramatic outcomes that aren't as random as one might initially believe. An inconsequential event in Brazil may have a dramatic impact on Texas.[6]

Scientists have coined this phenomenon as the butterfly effect, which underlies the foundation of chaos theory. Chaos theory refers to the seemingly paradoxical science of predicting unpredictable behavior. An experience may initially appear random, but it contains fundamental patterns and feedback loops, even when they aren't directly observable.

So, let's bring our focus to therapy. Let's say you are working in an inpatient facility with your client, Alex, a young man struggling with a serious opioid addiction. Alex has not experienced much success in therapy before. Everyone wants him to get sober. He also wants sobriety, but his extensive history of relapse has led him to feel relatively pessimistic about recovery.

Alex's body has detoxed from opioids, but his cravings are visceral. You don't always know exactly what to say or do, but you hold on to hope, and you show up with compassion and warmth. You don't give up on Alex, even though Alex has largely given up on himself.

Within the safety of your relationship, Alex feels encouraged to share more about his struggles and his desires to improve his life. He begins talking candidly about the hardships that led him to experiment with drugs in the first place. Slowly and cautiously, Alex stops using opioids altogether. They lose their powerful grip as he lifts his self-esteem and learns how to respond to challenging emotions differently.

Alex finishes treatment and relocates to another state for work. He thanks you for your support and for believing in his recovery. You wish him well and feel proud of his progress.

Many clients with addiction histories relapse. Alex has relapsed many times, but something is different in his recovery this time. He propels forward. He makes a genuine effort to start connecting with his loved ones, and he starts becoming the friend he always wanted to have. Some of his loved ones feel so inspired by Alex's changes that they apologize to the people they harmed. This domino effect plays out in relationships beyond Alex's direct social circle.

One night, Alex's friend, Jacob, calls him in a state of acute distress. Jacob is detoxing from heroin on his living room couch, but all he wants to do is get high. Alex drives over and spends the night with his struggling friend. The next morning, he sits with Jacob as they call different rehabilitation centers together. Two days later, Jacob is receiving inpatient care.

Two weeks later, while Jacob is in the bathroom between groups, he walks in on another client, Brad, who is overdosing. Jacob intervenes and ultimately saves Brad's life.

Several years later, inspired by these experiences, Alex becomes a therapist himself. His friend Jacob becomes a paramedic. Brad, humbled by his near-death experience, gets back together with the wife he almost left, which ultimately motivates her to seek recovery from her own addiction.

The above example may seem idealistic, but we have backgrounds in treating substance use disorders, and we have witnessed these types of amazing chain reactions occur often. The smallest shifts trigger immense reactions that can disrupt the status quo.

Even saying the chain of transformation started with Alex is too simplistic. What about you, the therapist, who believed in Alex's well-being and recovery? To take it even further, who molded and shaped you to care for your clients in the ways you did?

The virtues of one therapist's work can flow into the lives of so many people. The beauty is that this transcendence is constant, and it remains long after therapy ends. A butterfly flaps its wings. A therapist supports a client and believes in their recovery. The dice roll and set everything in motion. Every session and with every client.

You don't get to take every piece of the credit. The client, after all, does the work and makes the changes. You were just a butterfly. But look what a single butterfly can achieve.

We detest therapy books that contain only happily-ever-after endings, so we won't just stop with the Alex vignette. Treatment isn't always tied up neatly with a perfect bow. What about all those clients who don't get or stay sober? What about the many people who die from opioid overdoses? Did therapy make a difference for those clients?

This speaks to another dilemma. Horrible things happen to our clients. They lose their jobs or homes or dogs or sense of safety in the world. As a therapist, you sign up to sit with all this adversity. You may spend many sessions grappling with the unjust and unfair situations occurring in a client's life.

Therapy can't fix all the horrific problems in this world. Nothing can. This can never be the goal. You are not a savior; you do not read minds, and you can't perform magic. You can't even accurately predict what the future holds for your clients. You are a single entity existing within a gigantic system. The system will fail and traumatize many of your clients.

So, how can therapy matter when everything feels terrible? In so many ways, that's when it matters the most.

This is a job that calls for *trusting* that a client can always make changes, even if they don't believe anything can get better. This is a job that requires holding on to hope, even if everyone else has let it go. Sometimes, it's also about just bearing witness to indescribable pain. This way, your client doesn't have to be alone. Experiencing connectivity can't be overstated. While therapy doesn't always solve or fix, it can exquisitely convey, *No matter how bad or scary it is, I will still be here. I will hold this container for us.*

It is often said that therapists plant seeds with clients. By providing new insights or experiences, you offer a possibility for new outcomes. Sometimes, you get lucky—you have enough time with your client to really plant, water, and tend to those seeds well. You may be privileged to watch those first buds grow together.

At other times, life happens. In this age of managed care, other parties may dictate the length or capacity for treatment. You will not always see the full effects unfold. But years later, long after therapy ends, a beautiful tree might exist that didn't before. Sometimes. Not always. Nothing is guaranteed. You just offer the seeds.

EMBRACING THE CHAIN EFFECT OF CHANGE

Therapists put things in motion in many ways. The butterfly flaps its wings. A therapist helps a client make a single change. We are in the business of helping people become better versions of themselves. This can make the world a better place, continually and infinitely.

If you've been fortunate enough to receive meaningful therapy yourself, take a moment to consider the relevance of your own butterfly effect. How did the insights or experiences you gleaned in therapy change how you responded to the world around you? Maybe that change has encouraged you to be a gentler parent or a more emotionally present partner. Maybe it inspired you to engage in hobbies or creative activities that directly benefited other people.

The truth is that you may be impacting people you will never meet. You might also trigger events you will never know about.

For example, you teach one client a grounding exercise, and she shares it with a friend. That friend refers to that skill when she feels triggered to cut her thighs with a razor blade. You don't know your client's friend. You have never met her, you will never meet her, and you have no concept of her struggles or her attempts to work through them. However, the exercise you taught your client directly impacted how another person chose to cope at that moment.

You help someone else with their depression. They start to feel better, leading them to become more involved in local advocacy and charity work. Their benevolent actions improve the community, affecting hundreds of people you will never know.

This is what transcending sessions looks like. Your clients take the changes they receive from therapy into the world. When you can ground yourself in the magnitude of your work's meaning, you have a north star that can guide you when the days feel dreadful or challenging.

It's not always about perfect change or total healing. It's often about triggering the smallest shifts and disruptions.

And it doesn't always happen. Many clients will struggle. Some will leave treatment worse than when they entered it. It is normal to question whether any of this work makes a difference. This can be true for any industry, and if you sit with any healthcare professional, you'll hear similar conversations.

But it's important to pay attention to the shifts. Slight

changes can speak volumes, so allow yourself to witness those tiny transformations. Witness your clients gain more confidence and practice regulating their emotions. See how they set important boundaries that preserve their self-worth. Walk with them as they learn to let go of the habits that no longer serve them. And hold space and kindness when tough moments inevitably emerge.

Therapy helps clients feel more empowered to make choices that align with their values. With newfound strength, people can find their voices, and they can use those voices to change the world.

Our work can save lives. It can encourage people to be more honest, kinder, bolder, and braver. It can reduce abuse and open space for taboo fears and conversations and needs that have long needed to be addressed. It can and does break generational cycles.

It makes a difference, a monumental difference.

British psychoanalyst John Bowlby is widely quoted as saying, "Fortunately, the human psyche, like human bones, is strongly inclined towards self-healing." We have to believe in that. Even when our clients don't.

Your work can help clients, but it is so much greater than direct service work. If you are a therapist, you are ideally choosing to trust in humanity. This isn't about disregarding pain or embodying a mindset of toxic positivity. It's about believing that, at a cellular level, beauty within people exists. If you don't believe therapy makes a difference, if you don't believe people can genuinely grow and change, why should your clients? If you don't believe any of it matters, why should anyone?

And if we all collectively give up, *any* chance for systemic change is lost. Believing small movements make big differences underlies every social justice and charitable movement. To keep those movements afloat, hopelessness must be managed.

So, we hold on to hope and belief in therapy. We see how change happens, how it moves through couples and families and generations at large. We watch how entire systems progress and move. As mentioned, therapists don't get all the credit—our role is to support clients in becoming the best versions of themselves. And we believe that when people are operating better today than they were yesterday, the world changes. One butterfly at a time.

As one of our favorite therapists, Virginia Satir, once said, "I know people can change—right down to my bones, through every cell, in every fiber of my body—I know that people can change. It is just a question of when and in what context."[7]

You have to believe this work makes a difference. Bravely, fiercely, and without any doubt.

Finding Awe within the Connection

Genuinely meshing with people is one of the best parts of this work. There is immense joy in all forms of authentic human connection, even when that connection is professionally constrained.

Every session presents an opportunity to experience awe with clients. *Awe* refers to feeling wonder or reverence in a particular experience. It makes you feel that you are in the presence of something greater than yourself.

If you want to see awe in action, you just need to spend some time with small children. A baby is awed by their spinning mobile, and the toddler feels awe as they examine each petal of a sunflower. The world's youngest humans are bursting with awe, so much so that the adults around them often need to be reminded of the importance of staying present and slowing down.

A child doesn't choose to experience awe. It's innate to them.

Being a professional adult is nothing like being a toddling child collecting sticks. You can't suspend your critical thinking. You can't pretend the reality of this world doesn't exist. Work requires you to balance every competing demand. You have to think quickly. You have to make decisions that don't always feel fair. You have to manage clients at times when you feel tired, unsupported, bored, agitated, and more.

But you can still *choose* awe. Deliberately and frequently. Because doing so allows you to pour more energy into connecting, understanding, and helping your clients.

In therapy, awe lies in the heart of the relationships built with clients. Instead of viewing your sessions as tasks on a to-do list, you lean into vibrance. Like the toddling child exploring each crack on the sidewalk, you explore the feelings, sensations, needs, and inner experiences. By doing this, you sharpen your senses and slow down. With some clients, in some sessions, you will feel that undeniable zest and that full, glorious experience of *just being present*.

This matters. You find what makes your client wonderful. You internally remind yourself that there is nothing but what is arising in the here and now. In this space, the possibilities are endless. What you feel with and about this client is what exists. When you are here, you are just like that curious child, looking at every leaf with amazement.

It is here where scientists will talk about dopamine, the reward-driven neurotransmitter released during pleasurable moments, such as having sex, eating delicious meals, or watching a favorite movie. People are wired to seek dopamine, and from an evolutionary standpoint, it sustains human survival.

Oxytocin is a close cousin of dopamine and also induces pleasure, although that pleasure directly correlates with feeling connected to others. The brain secretes oxytocin during childbirth, breastfeeding, sex, and other forms of physical touch. People may also experience oxytocin during heightened moments of emotional connection, which might explain why bursting into laughter with friends or reading a heartfelt text from a partner feels so good. The emotional connectivity taps into the primal need for belongingness.

Embracing the core concepts discussed in this book can facilitate feelings of awe. By tending to your perfectionism or imposter syndrome, you create space for self-acceptance, mindfulness, and humanness. Using the skills referenced in the CHAIR framework allows you to deepen your relationships with clients. Tending to burnout addresses necessary pain points and opens you to feeling more refreshed in your work.

Therapy is packaged to be a one-sided relationship between therapist and client. It is advertised as a simple formula. Your client shares their problems and needs, and you integrate information to help them improve their emotional well-being.

From there, you initiate a transactional relationship constrained by professional boundaries. Depending on where you work, the relationship is also established and further defined by insurance standards, treatment goals, the length of a school semester, grant funds, and more. Whatever the case, your client will expose their vulnerabilities and needs, and you will strive to create a safe dynamic where insight can unfold and healing can take place.

But even if this relationship is entirely for the client's benefit (as it undoubtedly should be), the experience of co-creating this dynamic is not one-sided. You are always being affected. A client's experiences move you. You feel sad when they experience tragedy and loss. You share delight when meaningful success is achieved. You note a desire to protect when they are in immense pain.

Sometimes you also have those moments, those gorgeous and ineffable moments, when both you and your client feel completely harmonious. Renowned trauma expert Janina Fisher has exquisitely coined the term *attunement bliss* to describe the mutual attachment that can be felt between a parent and child.[8] This term holds similar clinical relevance between therapists and their clients.

Attunement bliss doesn't happen with every client or in every setting, and encountering it is not inherently necessary for successful treatment. But when you feel those moments of shared connection, the emotions are not one-sided either. You both share this wonder—the humanness of a transcendent experience is precisely what makes it so authentic and irreplaceable.

Therapists can really like or even love their clients. This love is different from romantically being in love; it's the felt love associated with being in a reciprocal state of shared warmth and emotional affection. In such a demanding line of work, this is such a wonderful virtue. Witnessing change and being a source of support to clients is a gift that should be deeply embraced.

When you generously give your clients the benefits of CHAIR—consistency, hope, attunement, impact, and repair— you offer them the healthy and compassionate relationship they deserve. In turn, you reap the pleasure of working with clients whose stories and personalities stay with you for the rest of your life.

In therapy, miracles can happen. In a book aimed to help

you love your career, it is worth emphasizing the beauty of building such dynamic relationships with others. It is an incredible honor worth treasuring.

As we wrote this section, we each spent time reflecting on the many clients and stories that moved us and changed us. Words can't accurately capture this type of privilege. We hope that you allow yourself to relish this kind of reflection from time to time. It gives our work a heartbeat.

We also spoke to many therapists about what keeps them feeling rejuvenated in their work. Many highlighted the relational aspect, as you can see below:

There is nothing more rewarding than helping a client start to feel a little better. Big changes matter, but when someone is severely depressed, the joy lives in those small breakthroughs. This is my purpose in life, and I don't deny myself the pleasure of celebrating my clients' wins with them.

My clients rarely trust people, including me. But, even long past the time they no longer need therapy, some of them request to continue on with our weekly appointments. We're connected, even if they still aren't sure about the whole therapy thing. They know I have their backs, and that feels good.

Nothing is more grounding than the relationships I have with my clients. I love them. Sincerely. I always wish them well.

It feels so good to get to care about people. I literally get paid to care about humanity.

It may be true that nobody is above the quest for dopamine. We're just instinctual humans wired to survive.

But it's more than that, isn't it? Because enjoying the

virtues of therapy is a gift for both clients and *you*. When both people look forward to the work and can savor each other's company, hope flourishes. Holding on to this very meaning can be what sustains you to keep showing up with love—day after day.

Human connection does not cure mental illness or solve emotional despair. But it can soften the edges of pain and open doors for empathy, validation, and shared understanding. The greatest healing happens through connection.

THE PRIVILEGE OF BEING A THERAPIST

There's a long-standing joke that therapists should never reveal their profession when people ask, "So, what do you do for a living?"

If you answer truthfully, you have opened the door for responses like "Oh no! Are you analyzing me right now?" or "Wow, you must really hear some crazy stories!" or "I have a question for you. . . . Can I ask you something about my brother's behavior?"

To avoid having to answer those questions, many therapists create cover stories. Maybe you opt for vagueness and tell people that you work in healthcare or another related industry. Maybe, to eliminate possible interrogation or commentary, you fabricate a new identity altogether.

The desire for anonymity makes sense. As we have mentioned, your career is not your identity, and it's healthy to separate your personal life from your job title. It can also be exhausting and even awkward to embody your professional presence in everyday interactions.

And yet.

We do not conceal our careers when asked what we do for a living. We are proud to be therapists. The privilege of having this role means we also welcome the inevitable conversations, criticism, and questions about therapy that come our way. Society is increasingly understanding the enormous gravity of mental health problems and how to treat them. We feel grateful for any opportunity to clarify misconceptions or validate fears about what we do.

So, why does this even matter?

We have devoted this book to highlighting the many difficulties therapists face in this career. But we have also sought to help therapists cultivate more acceptance, self-kindness, awareness, and love for what they do each day.

When you care about your work, you tend to feel proud of it. And when you feel proud of something, there's more weight, dimension, and purpose driving what you do. You protect what makes you proud. You *honor* what makes you proud.

And, as a bonus, those who embrace this profession nurture it. They move into advocacy. They fight for what's right in this occupation. They recognize the profession's limitations and manage its criticism constructively. They support continuous growth through research, treatment efforts, and system overhauls. They challenge stagnation and aim to leave this field better than how they entered it.

If you love and respect this work, you also give back to your colleagues. You are more apt to share resources and referrals. You are open to being a mentor or supervisor because you want to share insight and resources. This extends beyond direct therapy and moves into getting involved on societal levels, by donating to organizations that fund mental health treatment and backing politicians who support laws that strengthen healthcare accessibility. You campaign and protest and advocate for better rights for clients and their coworkers. Your passion for the work flows so much further than the singular sessions provided.

The work of therapy is arduous. The hours can be long, and the emotions can be restless, confusing, and unforgiving. Even if it is a labor of love, it's ignorant to underestimate the actual *labor* involved.

But the joy stands. It has to stand.

Therapy holds a mirror to all that is possible. It can and does change lives. It can and does spark dramatic movements, both on micro and macro levels. Witnessing someone's growth and development is one of the best parts of being human.

Therapy matters, and you as a therapist matter.

This job can truly be the privilege of a lifetime.

We are the lucky ones.

NOTES

1. HAS THE THERAPY PROFESSION FAILED YOU?

1. "Mental Health," World Health Organization, accessed June 29, 2024, https://www.who.int/health-topics/mental-health#tab=tab_1.
2. Parth Chodavadia, Irene Teo, Daniel Poremski, Daniel Shuen Sheng Fung, and Eric Andrew Finkelstein, "Prevalence and Economic Burden of Depression and Anxiety Symptoms among Singaporean Adults: Results from a 2022 Web Panel," *BMC Psychiatry* 23, no. 1 (2023): 104, https://doi.org/10.1186/s12888-023-04581-7.
3. "Suicide Statistics," Suicide Awareness Voices of Education (SAVE), accessed June 29, 2024, https://www.save.org/learn/suicide-statistics/#:~:text=In%202021%2C%2048%2C183%20Americans%20died,the%20US%20every%2010.9%20minutes.
4. "Data and Statistics on Children's Mental Health," Centers for Disease Control and Prevention, US Department of Health and Human Services, accessed June 29, 2024, https://www.cdc.gov/childrensmentalhealth/data.html.
5. "Scope of the Problem: Statistics," Rape, Abuse & Incest National Network (RAINN), accessed June 29, 2024, https://www.rainn.org/statistics/scope-problem.
6. Eric Graber, "Eating Disorders Are on the Rise," American Society for Nutrition, February 22, 2021, accessed June 29, 2024, https://nutrition.org/eating-disorders-are-on-the-rise/.
7. Megan Brenan, "Americans' Reported Mental Health at New Low; More Seek Help," Gallup, December 21, 2022, accessed June 29, 2024, https://news.gallup.com/poll/467303/americans-reported-mental-health-new-low-seek-help.aspx.

2. WHY DO YOU FEEL SO LOST IN YOUR CAREER?

1. Subway (@Subway), "We're excited to introduce our new [sandwich name]. Try it today!," September 17, 2018, Twitter (now X), accessed June 29, 2024, https://twitter.com/SUBWAY/status/1041763719766716417?lang=en.

2. Herbert A. Simon, "Rational Decision-Making in Business Organizations," Nobel Memorial Lecture, December 8, 1978, https://www.nobelprize.org/uploads/2018/06/simon-lecture.pdf.

3. Josh Wright, "What Is the Power of Regret? A Conversation with Daniel Pink," *Behavioral Scientist*, December 13, 2022, accessed June 29, 2024, https://behavioralscientist.org/what-is-the-power-of-regret-a-conversation-with-daniel-pink/.

4. Cheryl Strayed, "The Beauty of What Is," *Cheryl Strayed's Dear Sugar*, November 28, 2022, accessed July 27, 2024, https://cherylstrayed.substack.com/p/the-beauty-of-what-is.

5. Mark J. Perry, "Only 52 US Companies Have Been on the Fortune 500 since 1955, Thanks to the 'Creative Destruction' That Fuels Economic Prosperity," *Carpe Diem*, AEI, June 3, 2021, accessed June 29, 2024, https://www.aei.org/carpe-diem/only-52-us-companies-have-been-on-the-fortune-500-since-1955-thanks-to-the-creative-destruction-that-fuels-economic-prosperity-2/#:~:text=In%20other%20words%2C%20only%2010.4,from%20the%20top%20Fortune%20500.

3. WHAT IF YOU DON'T FEEL GOOD ENOUGH TO BE A THERAPIST?

1. Darshan H. Mehta, "Nurturing Resilience in the Wounded Healer," *Psychiatric Times*, January 9, 2024, accessed July 27, 2024, https://www.psychiatrictimes.com/view/nurturing-resilience-in-the-wounded-healer.

2. Harry Guntrip, "My Experience of Analysis with Fairbairn and Winnicott—(How Complete a Result Does Psycho-Analytic Therapy Achieve?)," *International Review of Psycho-Analysis* 2 (1975): 145–56, https://pep-web.org/search/document/IRP.002.0145A.

3. Benedict Carey, "Expert on Mental Illness Reveals Her Own Fight," *New York Times*, June 23, 2011, accessed June 29, 2024, https://www.nytimes.com/2011/06/23/health/23lives.html.

4. Phillip M. Kleespies, Kimberly A. Van Orden, Bruce Bongar, Diane Bridgeman, Lynn F. Bufka, Daniel I. Galper, Marc Hillbrand, and Robert I. Yufit, "Psychologist Suicide: Incidence, Impact, and Suggestions for Prevention, Intervention, and Postvention," *Professional Psychology: Research and Practice* 42, no. 3 (2011): 244–51, https://doi.org/10.1037/a0022805.

5. Katherine Morgan Schafler, *The Perfectionist's Guide to Losing Control: A Path to Peace and Power* (Portfolio/Penguin, 2023).

6. Kristin Neff, *Self-Compassion: The Proven Power of Being Kind to Yourself* (Hodder & Stoughton, 2011).

4. How Do You Strengthen Your Competence?

1. Scott Miller, Mark Hubble, and Barry Duncan, "The Secrets of Supershrinks: Pathways to Clinical Excellence," *Psychotherapy Networker: Clinical Guide*, 2014, accessed July 27, 2024, https://www.scottdmiller.com/wp-content/uploads/2014/06/Supershrinks-Free-Report-1.pdf.
2. Miller et al., "Supershrinks."
3. "Understanding Psychotherapy and How It Works," American Psychological Association, last updated December 12, 2023, accessed July 27, 2024, https://www.apa.org/topics/psychotherapy/understanding.
4. Malcolm Gladwell, *Outliers: The Story of Success* (Little, Brown, 2008).
5. K. Anders Ericsson and Kyle W. Harwell, "Deliberate Practice and Proposed Limits on the Effects of Practice on the Acquisition of Expert Performance: Why the Original Definition Matters and Recommendations for Future Research," *Frontiers in Psychology* 10 (October 24, 2019), accessed July 27, 2024, https://www.frontiersin.org/journals/psychology/articles/10.3389/fpsyg.2019.02396/full.
6. Terence Tracey, James Lichtenberg, Rod Goodyear, and Bruce Wampold, "Do Therapists Get Better with Experience?," chap. 17 in *APA Handbook of Psychotherapy: Evidence-Based Practice, Practice-Based Evidence, and Contextual Participant-Driven Practice*, vol. 2 (Washington, DC: American Psychological Association, 2023), January 2024, https://www.researchgate.net/publication/377040929_Do_therapists_get_better_with_experience.
7. Miller et al., "Supershrinks."
8. Jon Frederickson, "How Do Experts Become Competent?," Deliberate Practice in Psychotherapy, accessed July 27, 2024, https://deliberatepracticeinpsychotherapy.com/wp-content/uploads/2017/02/DL2.pdf.
9. Daryl Chow, "Clinical Practice vs. Deliberate Practice: Why Your Years of Experience Doesn't Get You Better," Frontiers of Psychotherapist Development, January 17, 2015, updated February 10, 2021, accessed July 27, 2024, https://darylchow.com/frontiers/clinical-practice-vs-deliberate-practice/#:~:text=Said%20another%20way%2C%20clini-cal,let%20go%20all%20of%20that.
10. Miller et al., "Supershrinks."

5. What Do Clients Value Most from Therapy?

1. Soo Kim, "How Finding 'Glimmers' of Hope in Day to Day Life Improves Mental Health," *Newsweek*, July 23, 2023, accessed July 27, 2024, https://

www.newsweek.com/mental-health-crisis-glimmers-trauma-therapy-viral-tiktok-1814542.

2. Megan Call, "Neuroplasticity: How to Use Your Brain's Malleability to Improve Your Well-Being," University of Utah Health, *Accelerate,* August 8, 2019, accessed June 29, 2024, https://accelerate.uofuhealth.utah.edu/resilience/neuroplasticity-how-to-use-your-brain-s-malleability-to-improve-your-well-being.

3. Karen Hopenwasser, "Being in Rhythm: Dissociative Attunement in Therapeutic Process," *Journal of Trauma & Dissociation* 9, no. 3 (2008): 349–67, https://www.tandfonline.com/doi/abs/10.1080/15299730802139212.

4. Franz Alexander, Thomas Morton French, et al., chap. 2 in *Psychoanalytic Therapy: Principles and Application* (Ronald Press, 1946).

5. Linda Finlay, "Theory: Empathic Attunement and Transference in Kohut's Self-Psychology," chap. 4 in *Relational Integrative Psychotherapy: Process and Theory in Practice* (Chichester, England: Wiley, 2015), accessed June 29, 2024, http://relational-integrative-psychotherapy.uk/wp-content/uploads/2015/02/Chapter-4-Kohut-Theory-handout.pdf.

6. Richard G. Erskine, Janet P. Moursund, and Rebecca L. Trautmann, *Beyond Empathy: A Therapy of Contact-in-Relationship* (New York: Routledge, 1999).

7. Peter Fonagy and Elizabeth Allison, "What Is Mentalization? The Concept and Its Foundations in Developmental Research and Social-Cognitive Neuroscience," 2011, https://discovery.ucl.ac.uk/id/eprint/1430329/7/Fonagy_chapter1_draft_pfrevised_protected.pdf.

8. Ellen Galinsky, "PBS's 'This Emotional Life': The Magic of Relationships," HuffPost, July 9, 2010, updated November 17, 2011, accessed June 29, 2024, https://www.huffpost.com/entry/pbss-this-emotional-life_b_568178.

6. What Makes Therapy Impactful?

1. Matt Blanchard and Barry A. Farber, "Lying in Psychotherapy: Why and What Clients Don't Tell Their Therapist about Therapy and Their Relationship," *Counselling Psychology Quarterly* 29, no. 1 (2016): 90–112, https://doi.org/10.1080/09515070.2015.1085365.

2. Laura Zimmerman, "Deception Detection," American Psychological Association, *Monitor on Psychology* 47, no. 3 (March 2016): 46, accessed June 29, 2024, https://www.apa.org/monitor/2016/03/deception.

3. Robert Duesler, *Therapist Self-Disclosure as a Psychotherapy Technique,* December 2020, accessed June 29, 2024, https://www.researchgate.net/publication/353304451_Therapist_Self-Disclosure_as_a_Psychotherapy_Technique.

4. Jennifer R. Henretty and Heidi M. Levitt, "The Role of Therapist Self-Disclosure in Psychotherapy: A Qualitative Review," *Clinical Psychology Review* 30, no. 1 (February 2010): 63–77, accessed June 29, 2024, https://www.sciencedirect.com/science/article/abs/pii/S0272735809001354#:~:text=Over%2090%25%20of%20therapists%20-self,one%20study%20to%20the%20next.
5. "Understanding the Johari Window Model," Selfawareness.org.uk, accessed June 29, 2024, https://selfawareness.org.uk/2022/09/25/understanding-the-johari-window-model/.

7. What If You Make a Mistake with a Client?

1. Jeremy D. Safran, J. Christopher Muran, and Alexandra Shaker, "Research on Therapeutic Impasses and Ruptures in the Therapeutic Alliance," *Contemporary Psychoanalysis* 50, no. 1–2 (April 2014): 211–32, accessed June 29, 2024, https://www.tandfonline.com/doi/abs/10.1080/00107530.2014.880318.
2. Jacob Goldsmith, "The Value of Difficult Moments in the Client-Therapist Relationship," Family Institute at Northwestern University, *Clinical Science Insights*, 2013, https://www.family-institute.org/sites/default/files/pdfs/csi_goldsmith_therapist_relationship.pdf.
3. Jeremy D. Safran, Peter Crocker, Shelly McMain, and Paul Murray, "Therapeutic Alliance Rupture as a Therapy Event for Empirical Investigation," *Psychotherapy: Theory, Research, Practice, Training* 27, no. 2 (1990): 154–65, https://doi.org/10.1037/0033-3204.27.2.154.

8. How Do You Maintain Compassion and Respect for Your Clients?

1. Friedrich Nietzsche, *Beyond Good and Evil* (Dover Publications, 1998).

10. What If You're Burnt Out?

1. Nicole Arzt, *Sometimes Therapy Is Awkward: A Collection of Life-Changing Insights for the Modern Clinician* (Soul of Therapy, 2020).
2. Alok Patel and Stephanie Plowman, "The Increasing Importance of a Best Friend at Work," Gallup Workplace, August 17, 2022, updated January 19, 2024, accessed July 27, 2024, https://www.gallup.com/workplace/397058/increasing-importance-best-friend-work.aspx.
3. Amy Wrzesniewski and Jane E. Dutton, "Crafting a Job: Revisioning Employees as Active Crafters of Their Work," *Academy of Management Review* 26, no. 2 (2001): 179–201, accessed July 27, 2024, https://

positiveorgs.bus.umich.edu/wp-content/uploads/Crafting-a-Job_Revisioning-Employees.pdf.

11. SHOULD YOU QUIT YOUR JOB?

1. Equal Pay Day: March 12, 2024," US Census Bureau, March 12, 2024, accessed July 27, 2024, https://www.census.gov/newsroom/stories/equal-pay-day.html.

12. WHAT'S IN IT FOR YOU?

1. Erin M. Fekete and Nathan T. Deichert, "A Brief Gratitude Writing Intervention Decreased Stress and Negative Affect during the COVID-19 Pandemic," *Journal of Happiness Studies* 23, no. 6 (February 24, 2022): 2427–48, doi: 10.1007/s10902-022-00505-6, accessed July 27, 2024,https://www.ncbi.nlm.nih.gov/pmc/articles/PMC8867461/.
2. Martin A. Nowak and Sébastien Roch, "Upstream Reciprocity and the Evolution of Gratitude," *Proceedings of the Royal Society B: Biological Sciences* 274, no. 1610 (March 7, 2007): 605–10, doi: 10.1098/rspb.2006.0125, accessed July 27, 2024, https://www.ncbi.nlm.nih.gov/pmc/articles/PMC2197219/.
3. Joanna Tomczyk, Izabela Krejtz, Monika Kornacka, and John B. Nezlek, "A Grateful Disposition Promotes the Well-Being of Women with Breast Cancer through Adaptive Coping," *International Journal of Women's Health* 13 (June 16, 2021): 579–90, doi: 10.2147/IJWH.S294216, accessed July 27, 2024, https://www.ncbi.nlm.nih.gov/pmc/articles/PMC8215929/.
4. Hong Chen, Xiujuan Yang, Wei Xia, Yunduan Li, YaLing Deng, and Cuiying Fan, "The Relationship between Gratitude and Job Satisfaction: The Mediating Roles of Social Support and Job Crafting," *Current Psychology* 42, no. 3 (March 30, 2021), doi:10.1007/s12144-021-01658-y, accessed July 27, 2024, https://www.researchgate.net/publication/350498976_The_relationship_between_gratitude_and_job_satisfaction_The_mediating_roles_of_social_support_and_job_crafting.
5. Alexandra P. Townsley, Jenny Li-Wang, and Rajani Katta, "Healthcare Workers' Well-Being: A Systematic Review of Positive Psychology Interventions," *Cureus* 15, no. 1 (January 23, 2023): e34102, doi:10.7759/cureus.34102, accessed July 27, 2024, https://www.ncbi.nlm.nih.gov/pmc/articles/PMC9946896/.
6. Edward N. Lorenz, "Predictability: Does the Flap of a Butterfly's Wings in Brazil Set Off a Tornado in Texas?," paper presented before the American Association for the Advancement of Science, December 29, 1972, *Hvad er matematik? B, i-bog*, ISBN: 978 87 7066 494 3, Hjemmesidehenvisning

ABOUT THE AUTHORS

Nicole Arzt, LMFT, is an author, speaker, and practicing psychotherapist. She specializes in treating complex trauma and all substance use disorders, with a focus on supporting newer therapists. She has previous experience working in school-based settings, hospitals, nonprofit healthcare, and inpatient mental health treatment. Nicole is the founder and owner of Soul of Therapy LLC, a boutique media business for therapists. Her writing has been featured in *Forbes, Yahoo! News*, the *Today* show, and more. In 2018, Nicole founded @psychotherapymemes, a global community dedicated to bringing humor and lightness into this heavy profession. Learn more at www.nicolearzt.com.

Jeremy Arzt, LMFT, is a clinical supervisor and practicing psychotherapist. He specializes in treating attachment trauma, men's issues, and couples. In his former role as chief clinical officer, he managed multidisciplinary clinical duties for several inpatient and outpatient mental health programs throughout Southern California. Jeremy also has previous faculty experience teaching family therapy and trauma courses for graduate students. He currently facilitates attachment-based consultation groups for mental health professionals and offers depth-oriented supervision for training therapists. Learn more at www.jeremyarzt.com.

Printed in the USA
CPSIA information can be obtained
at www.ICGtesting.com
CBHW061513081024
15567CB00027B/607